D0792963

Adoption across Borders

Serving the Children in Transracial and Intercountry Adoptions

Rita J. Simon
and
Howard Altstein

ROWMAN & LITTLEFIELD PUBLISHERS, INC.
Lanham • Boulder • New York • Oxford

ROWMAN & LITTLEFIELD PUBLISHERS, INC.

Published in the United States of America
by Rowman & Littlefield Publishers, Inc.
4720 Boston Way, Lanham, Maryland 20706
http://www.rowmanlittlefield.com

12 Hid's Copse Road
Cumnor Hill, Oxford OX2 9JJ, England

British Library Cataloguing in Publication Information Available

Library of Congress Cataloging-in-Publication Data

Simon, Rita James.
    Adoption across borders : serving the children in transracial and
intercountry adoptions
    / Rita J. Simon and Howard Altstein.
        p.   cm.
    Includes bibliographical references and index.
    ISBN 0-8476-9832-7 (cloth : alk. paper)—ISBN 0-8476-9833-5 (pbk. : alk.
paper)
        1. Interracial adoption—United States.   2. Intercountry adoption—
United States.—I. Altstein, Howard.   II. Title.
    HV875.64.S555   2000
    362.73'4—dc21   99-049163

Printed in the United States of America

∞ ™ The paper used in this publication meets the minimum requirements of
American National Standard for Information Sciences—Permanence of Paper
for Printed Library Materials, ANSI Z39.48-1992.

Adoption across Borders

For our grandchildren
Audrey Altstein Bachman
and
Charlotte Mae and Julian Lincoln Garrett

Contents

Preface

Culminating from research that the authors began in 1971, this volume describes the findings and evaluations of the major studies on transracial and intercountry adoptions over the past thirty years. It also provides a brief history and the best estimates of the frequencies of transracial and intercountry adoptions in the United States and includes an overview of the debate surrounding the practices, policies, and legal issues. It presents a summary of federal and state statutes for transracial adoptions in the United States, as well as a review of international laws and conventions as they bear on adopting children into the United States from abroad.

This volume describes and compares the findings of the Simon-Altstein twenty-year longitudinal study conducted from 1970 through 1992 of transracial adoptees, over two-thirds of whom were African-American children, against a 1994 study of adolescent and adult Korean adoptees and their white parents. It also compares the results of two surveys of white Jewish parents who belong to the Stars of David and their experiences with African-American, Hispanic, Korean, and other intercountry adoptees in 1987 and again in 1997. (The "Stars of David" is a Boston-based, nationwide adoptive parent group. See chapter 7 for a description of the organization and its practices.) In the twenty-year study, the Korean survey, and the first of the two Stars of David surveys, the parents as well as the adoptees were interviewed;

and in the twenty-year study, birth children were also interviewed. In the second Stars of David survey, only the parents were interviewed.

Readers looking for a discussion of some of the other contentious and pressing issues confronting adoptions generally will need to look elsewhere, as this volume does not enter the debates that focus on open adoptions, subsidized adoptions, single-parent adoptions, open records, adoption by gay parents, and adoptees' right to know.

Chapter 1, "The History and Frequency of Transracial and Intercountry Adoptions," provides a brief history of transracial and intercountry adoptions, including an estimate of the number of transracial adoptions from the late 1960s and a count of the number of children adopted by American parents from outside the United States. The frequencies are provided by the countries involved, along with the policies adopted by the sending countries from the 1950s to the present.

Chapter 2, "The Legal Perspective on Transracial and Intercountry Adoptions," presents a review of the state statutes and the case law bearing on transracial and intercountry adoptions. The 1994 Multi-Ethnic Placement Act, the 1997 Adoption and Safe Families Act, and the 1978 Indian Child Welfare Act are discussed for their impact on transracial adoptions. For intercountry adoptions, the U.S. immigration law, international treaties, and accounts of the Hague Convention for the Protection of Children are reported.

Chapter 3, "The Case against Transracial Adoption," focuses on a discussion of the controversies surrounding transracial adoption. The National Association of Black Social Workers traditionally opposed transracial adoption, though their position has evolved from referring to the practice as racial genocide to advocating family preservation and transracial adoption as a last alternative.

Chapter 4, "Results of Empirical Studies of Transracial Adoptions," begins with a discussion of the work of David Fanshel in the 1960s on the transracial adoption of American-Indian children and continues with the work of Lucille Grow and Deborah Shapiro of the Child Welfare League. The chapter reviews key empirical work that has been conducted on transracial adoptions and includes an account of the Simon-Altstein Twenty-Year Study of white parents who adopted minority children, which began in 1971 and continued through 1992.

Chapter 5, "Results of Empirical Studies of Intercountry Adoptions," reviews empirical studies of children who were adopted from overseas into the United States. Most of the studies evaluate the success of Korean adoptees in the 1970s, '80s, and '90s. The chapter includes a survey conducted by the authors in 1993 of adult Korean adoptees and their white American parents.

Chapter 6, "A Comparison of the Experiences of Adult Korean and Black Transracial Adoptees," features a comparison of the responses of the parents and the adoptees to the adult Koreans; the fourth phase of the Simon-Altstein twenty-year study is also discussed. The survey instruments used in the two studies were almost identical.

Chapter 7, "The Experiences of Stars of David Families: 1987 and 1997," contains a report of two surveys conducted ten years apart of families who belong to the Stars of David. The Stars of David is a national Jewish parent network, composed of families who have adopted children across racial and national lines.

Chapter 8, "Concluding Remarks," gives a summary of the prior chapters, plus policy recommendations and a discussion of the relationship between welfare policies and adoption practices.

1

✛

The History and Frequency of Transracial and Intercountry Adoptions

The origins of transracial adoption (TRA) can be traced to the activities of the Children's Service Center and a group of parents in Montreal, Quebec, Canada, who in 1960 founded an organization known as the Open Door Society. The Children's Service Center sought placement for black children among Canada's black community. It worked with black community leaders and the media to find black homes for these children. It was unsuccessful. The Center then turned to its list of white adoptive parents, and the first transracial adoptions were made. Between 1951 and 1963, five black and sixty-six biracial Canadian children were transracially adopted by white families.

In the United States, 1961 marked the founding in Minnesota of Parents to Adopt Minority Youngsters (PAMY). PAMY was one of the first groups in this country to be formed along the lines of the Open Door Society in Canada, with similar referral, recruitment, and public relations practices. PAMY's involvement with transracial adoption, like that of the Open Door Society, came as an unexpected by-product of its original unsuccessful attempt to secure black adoptive homes for

1

black children. From 1962 through 1965, approximately twenty black children in Minnesota were adopted by white families through the efforts of PAMY.[1] By 1969, forty-seven organizations similar to the Open Door Society were operating in the United States.[2]

But enthusiasm for transracial adoptions was short-lived. In 1972, the National Association of Black Social Workers (NABSW) issued TRA's death warrant with its resolution calling transracial adoption "[a] particular form of genocide." Agencies were quick to fall in line with the NABSW. In the years immediately preceding that resolution, 2,274 black children were adopted by white families in 1970, 2,574 were adopted in 1971, and 1,569 were adopted in 1972. But 1973 saw only a little more than 1,000 black children adopted by white families.[3] The Child Welfare League of America (CWLA), in its *Standards for Adoption Practice,* implemented the NABSW's position by changing its view from "racial background in itself should not determine the selection of a home for a child"[4] to "children placed with adoptive families with similar racial characteristics can become more easily integrated into the average family and community."[5]

By 1976 transracial adoption as a serious alternative for moving black children out of institutions and foster care was just about over.[6] The rare arguments in favor of TRA still defined it as "second best" to permanent inracial placement or included strong support for community agencies to vigorously recruit minority adoptive parents. In its 1988 *Standards for Adoption Service* (despite all the changes that have occurred in adoption since 1988, this almost twelve-year-old document stands as the "latest revision"), the Child Welfare League reaffirmed that transracial adoptions should be considered only after all efforts at inracial placement have been exhausted. Under the title "Factors in Selection of Family: Ethnicity and Race," the *Standards* read:

> Children in need of adoption have a right to be placed into a family that reflects their ethnicity or race. Children should not have their adoption denied or significantly delayed, however, when adoptive parents of other ethnic or racial groups are available.[7]

> In any adoption plan, however, the best interests of the child should be paramount. If aggressive, ongoing recruitment efforts are unsuccessful

in finding families of the same ethnicity or culture, other families should be considered.[8]

The development of transracial adoption did not result from deliberate agency programming but from an accommodation to perceived reality. Social changes regarding abortion, contraception, single parenthood, and reproduction in general had reduced the number of white children available for adoption, leaving nonwhite children as the largest available source. Changes also occurred regarding the willingness of white couples to adopt nonwhite children.

Those originally opposed to transracial adoption challenged the two main assumptions upon which it was founded: first, that there are insufficient black parents willing to adopt black children, and second, that the benefits a black child will receive in a white family surpass those received in any temporary placement. In 1999, TRA continues to be opposed on similar grounds, although with the passage of the 1997 Adoption and Safe Families Act opposition should not have real effect. But from the mid-1970s up to the passage of the 1997 Act, most agencies were unwilling to place black children with white families, and opponents of TRA continued to argue that the ratio between adoptable black children and available black homes was artificially deflated as a result of racism. In other words, opponents of TRA continued to state that white-controlled adoption agencies make conscious efforts not to involve the black community more fully in attempting to recruit black adoptive parents.

Adoption agencies exercised almost total control in establishing, maintaining, and enforcing what can be termed a "virtuous scale," a list of characteristics thought to be predictive of success in adoptive parenting. These characteristics included such factors as age, years married, religion (and religiosity), income, physical and mental health, and infertility.[9]

In many cases the racial composition of the agency, its administrators, and its social workers determined the extent to which transracial placements were seen as an appropriate social work goal. For example, a 1991 report by the North American Council on Adoptable Children described rates of transracial placements in agencies in which white professionals were in the majority as compared to minority-staffed agencies. The latter placed only 6 percent of all nonwhite children transracially; the former placed 50 percent of their Hispanic children transracially.[10]

With the passage of years, adoption practice in the United States has dramatically changed. Agencies no longer wield the almost-exclusive control they once did because there is a severe dearth of adoptable children—more accurately, a scarcity of healthy white infants. Curiously, only in transracial adoption do agencies retain any sort of power—power that is utilized in most cases to prevent such placements.

ADOPTION STATISTICS

The federal government began collecting national adoption figures in 1944, but it has not gathered such data since 1975, a year in which 129,000 adoptions occurred, of which 831 were transracial.

To this date (1999), we remain without comprehensive official statistics on adoption. Even the 1975 figures cited previously were incomplete, in that they represented only twenty-three states and excluded some of the largest. To remedy this important gap in national adoption statistics, Congress mandated their resumption as of October 1991. It is now spring 1999, and we are still without these data. Yet some other data are available.

The following statistics are approximate 1999 figures that we believe are relevant to transracial adoption:

(1) There are anywhere from 450,000 to 500,000 children in America's foster care system, about 40 to 50 percent of whom are black.[11] In 1992 there were about 429,000 children in foster care, an increase of 53 percent from 1987.[12]

(2) There are about 50,000 children legally free for adoption, many of whom have special needs (physically/emotionally handicapped, sibling groups, older, nonwhite). This figure rises to about 85,000 children if the formula used by many states is taken into account—

namely, that about 20 percent of all foster care children eventually have adoption as a casework goal.[13]

(3) The figures in table 1.1 represent all adoptions for the years 1987, 1990, and 1992. Percent of change is indicated. Adoptions are not classified by related and unrelated. The latter are nonrelative adoptions. Related adoptions are usually step-parent and relative adoptions. In most years these are approximately equally divided. For example, in 1986 related adoptions accounted for 50.9 percent of all adoptions. Unrelated adoptions equaled the remainder, 49.1 percent.[14]

(4) TRA figures are extremely hard to come by. We have no way of knowing actual numbers, but most observers would agree that actual numbers are very small. For example, in analyzing 1987 data it was found that "92 percent of all adoptions involve an adoptive mother and child of the same race. . . . In only 8 percent of all adoptions are the parents and children of different races."[15] But this does not mean that 8 percent of all adoptions in the United States were TRAs. Included in this figure are thousands of intercountry adoptions (ICA); "the actual incidence of TRA among children born in the U.S. may be very low indeed."[16] In fact, the 1987 TRA figure for black children adopted by white families may be as low as 1.2 percent.[17] There is no reason to believe this figure is any different in 1999.

It is ironic that we have precise figures on how many foreign-born orphans are adopted by Americans but such unreliable figures on how many American children are adopted by Americans.

INTERCOUNTRY ADOPTIONS

Intercountry adoptions (ICA) began as a philanthropic endeavor at the end of World War II in Europe. But ICA is not a European story. It is

Table 1.1   All Adoptions per Year

1987[a]	1990[a]	1992[b]	% Change 1987–1990	% Change 1990–1992
117,585	118,779	128,000	+1.0	+7.7

[a]"Adoption Statistics by State," Victor Eugene Flango and Carol R. Flango, *Child Welfare*, CWLA, vol. 72, no. 3 (May–June, 1993): 311–19.
[b]Interview with staffer, U.S. House of Representatives, Ways and Means Committee.

a global tale that saw Europe change from a continent that supplied parentless children to the United States to one that today rivals the United States in receiving orphans from other lands. In 1999, ICA is a story of global race relations, where nonwhite, free-for-adoption Third World children are adopted by white families living in the West.

Since the end of World War II, hundreds of thousands of families in the United States, Western Europe, Canada, Oceania, and Israel have adopted non-native-born nonwhite children. Between 1953 and 1962, approximately 15,000 foreign-born children were adopted by American families. The following eleven years, 1965–1976, saw an additional 37,469 foreign-born children adopted, of which about 65 percent came from Asia, mostly from the Republic of Korea (ROK). The years from 1977 to 1983 saw an additional 39,555 non-U.S.-born orphans adopted in the United States, 55 percent of whom were Korean-born.

Table 1.2 shows the number of intercountry adoptions from 1989 through 1998 by country of birth.

The variation in the number of intercountry adoptees during the ten-year interval described in table 1.2, from a low of 6,536 in 1992 to a high of 15,774 in 1998, can be explained almost completely by looking at the number of Asian (and, as shown in table 1.3, these are over-

Table 1.2 Number of Intercountry Adoptions by Region, 1989–1998

Year	Europe	Asia	Africa	Oceania	North America	South America	Total All Regions
1989	120	5,112	36	13	910	1,757	7,948
1990	232	3,823	49	11	1,016	1,957	7,088
1991	2,761	3,194	41	16	1,047	1,949	9,008
1992	874	3,032	63	13	1,136	1,418	6,536
1993	1,521	3,163	59	1	1,133	1,471	7,348
1994	2,370	3,687	83	8	847	1,205	8,200
1995	2,660	4,843	104	9	764	1,004	9,384
1996	3,568	6,100	89	4	750	805	11,316
1997	5,176	6,483	182	4	1,228	548	13,620
1998	5,660	7,827	172	4	1,456	655	15,774

Source: U.S. Department of State and Immigration and Naturalization Service. Reported in "The Bulletin of the Joint Council on International Children's Services," (Spring 1999); and *http://www.travel.state.gov/orphan_html* "Immigration Visas Issued to Orphans Coming to U.S."

whelmingly Korean children) children allowed to be adopted in the United States. In 1989 that figure was 5,112; by 1992 it dropped to 1,787.

ASIAN INTERCOUNTRY ADOPTIONS

Republic of Korea

The Republic of Korea (ROK) has historically supplied the United States and the West with the majority of their intercountry adoptees. ROK is a Confucian society where bloodlines and family heritage are the defining characteristics in establishing an individual's identity. It is also a society where adoption as we know it in the West (of non-blood-related orphans) never existed until recently, when attempts were made to introduce this concept. Historically, the extended family assumed a caretaker responsibility for parentless children.[18] Over-whelmingly, this was done to preserve property rights and bloodlines. Maintaining the viability of the extended family's bloodlines is probably the single most important reason to explain relatives' caretaker function for orphaned progeny. Several major events occurred as a result of the Korean War, however, that helped transform the way Korean society cared for its orphans. These events include: (1) large population shifts from rural to urban areas; (2) a breakdown of the extended family; (3) large numbers of orphaned children, many of whom were "illegitimate"; and (4) an influx of Western ideas, values, and social institutions. To cope with the staggering number of parentless children, the Republic of Korea, with the assistance and encouragement of American social welfare agencies, began to send its orphans to the West, especially to the United States.

From the 1950s until the early 1970s, Korea was the main provider of infants to the West. For some thirty years Korea allowed thousands of its orphaned children to be adopted by foreigners. Although no exact figures exist, it is estimated that between the early 1950s and the mid-1980s, in excess of 100,000 Korean-born children were adopted by Western families.[19] Table 1.3 describes the total number of adoptions from all Asian nations.

Table 1.3   Total Adoptions from Asia, 1989–1998

Year	China (PRC)	China (ROC)	Hong Kong	All China*	ROK	Asia	All Regions
1989	33	62	47	142	3,552	5,112	7,948
1990	28	66	37	131	2,603	3,823	7,088
1991	62	55	40	157	1,817	3,194	9,008
1992	201	35	27	263	1,787	3,032	6,536
1993	330	31	27	388	1,765	3,163	7,348
1994	748	34	27	809	1,757	3,687	8,200
1995	2,049	23	26	2,098	1,570	4,843	9,384
1996	3,313	21	29	3,363	1,580	6,100	11,316
1997	3,597	19	21	3,637	1,654	6,483	13,621
1998	4,206	30	27	4,263	1,829	7,827	15,774

Source: U.S. Department of State and Immigration and Naturalization Service. Reported in the "Bulletin of the Joint Council on International Children's Services" (Spring 1999); and *http://www.travel.state.gov/orphan_html* "Immigrant Visas Issued to Orphans Coming to U.S."
*People's Republic of China, Republic of China, Hong Kong

But, as witnessed by the figures in table 1.3, since 1988 the Republic of Korea began to reduce the number of children it allowed to be adopted by foreigners. Although in 1994 Asia remained the leading supplier of children to the United States, with the Republic of Korea providing the largest number, the numbers of Korean children fell considerably. Whereas ROK led all Asian countries in 1989, with 3,552 orphans sent to the United States (of 7,948 Asian children), by 1995 only 1,570 ROK orphans were adopted by U.S. citizens.

Of the 7,827 Asian children adopted by U.S. families in 1998, China provided the most children (4,206, or 54 percent) and Korea provided some 23 percent. In 1998 Korea increased the number of children it allowed U.S. families to adopt, but it remained behind China, which also increased its number.[20]

The reasons for Korea's reduction have to do with national pride and the fact that Korea no longer is considered a developing country incapable of caring for its own. By the end of the twentieth century, Korea has become a major economic force in the world's markets, rich enough to provide for its own orphans. Nationalism and economics are twin factors in sharply reducing the number of Korean children sent abroad for adoption.[21]

Important, too, in reducing the numbers of Korean children adopted by Westerners was a 1980 statute liberalizing the availability of abortion services in the Republic of Korea. The legalization of abortion has had some impact, but other, more powerful, factors also affect the reduction, not the least of which is North Korea's constant haranguing that by "selling" its children to the West, the Republic of Korea is engaging in capitalism at its worst.[22] In 1993 an official in the ROK's Health Ministry was quoted as saying:

> We are going to stop foreign adoption by 1996, although this will not include the handicapped. We believe we will by then be able to take care of our own children.[23]

China

With a population of 1.3 billion people, much attention has been given to the People's Republic of China (PRC) as one of America's main suppliers of adoptable orphans.[24] As seen in table 1.3, in 1989 the PRC allowed only 33 of its children to be adopted in the United States. In fact, from 1989 to 1991 the PRC allowed only 123 of its orphans to be adopted by American parents. The year 1988 began a period of "ups" and "downs" in the number of Chinese-born orphans whom U.S. citizens were allowed to adopt. But 1992 saw the start of a sustained period of intercountry adoption. By 1998 China had become our largest supplier of Asian-born adoptees, with 4,206 children. As the twentieth century closes, adoption of Chinese orphans is one of the most preferred forms of intercountry adoption.

Why did the number of orphans from the PRC increase so dramatically from 1989 to 1998, a ten-year period? Aside from the fact that, historically, China (as is the case with all Asian societies) has almost no history of domestic adoption, most observers point to the PRC's one-child policy as the main reason why so many children were abandoned, with the lucky few being selected for intercountry adoption. A typical scenario to explain the large numbers of adoptable Chinese children would go something like this: Since a Chinese family is limited to having only one child or else must suffer severe punishments, most people still prefer that child to be male. (In fact, males remain the preferred gender in most of Asia.) If a female is born to Chinese parents, they will relinquish her to a state-operated orphanage and will try to conceive again, hoping for a male. They might surrender (or kill) as many females as they have until a male is born.

Another explanation for the appearance of so many Chinese orphans could be: money. China receives valuable Western currency (an average of $15,000 per adoption, including a donation to the child's orphanage of $3,000) by allowing the best of its orphans to be adopted.[25] Those not selected for adoption in the West are, for the most part, children who are handicapped or otherwise physically unattractive. They are categorized as "unadoptable" and left to their fate in state orphanages. Although "unadoptable" is somewhat less pejorative than the category of "irretrievable," the term used by Romanian child-welfare personnel to describe less-than-perfect orphans, for the children so labeled the consequences are similar and, as some report, tragic.

In 1996, Human Rights Watch/Asia published a report entitled *Death by Default: A Policy of Fatal Neglect in China's State Orphanages.* The report described the systematic abuse and killing of Chinese orphans, mostly unwanted and abandoned females and handicapped children. According to Human Rights Watch/Asia, killings occurred in state-operated orphanages from the late 1980s until the early 1990s. Articles appeared in the press, supporting the allegations of Human Rights Watch. The *Baltimore Sun* reported that orphans were deprived of medical attention and allowed to die of starvation.[26] The *New York Times* wrote that the death rate in some state-run orphanages was as high as 50 percent; in others, it was close to 90 percent.[27]

Some Westerners suggest that the problem of abuse and neglect in China's orphanages is overstated, that orphans living in institutions throughout the developing world experience similar conditions as those described in the Human Rights Watch report. A few responded to the report by saying that the conditions described are no worse than those many American children experience in foster care in the United States.[28] Also, a coalition of Chinese authorities, Western adoption agencies, and adoptive parent groups repudiated the Human Rights Watch report, adding that its findings were not independently verified.[29]

In fact, some critics went further. In a National Public Radio story on March 20, 1996, Rene Montagne interviewed a policy researcher on China (Kay Johnson, Hampshire College), a clergyman familiar with China, and an ICA expert knowledgeable about China's adoption policies (Susan Cox, Holt International). All of the individuals interviewed suggested that the Human Rights Watch document was exaggerated. One person said that the report was based on the statements of one physician located in one orphanage in Shanghai, concerning events that occurred from 1988 to 1992. There is no "government policy to exterminate children," said one of the interviewees. Professor Johnson explained that many times hospitals send their terminally ill children to orphanages to await death, as if orphanages and hospices were synonymous. This perhaps explains many of the reported orphanage deaths.

The real fear on the part of potential adopters and adoption agencies is that the PRC will retaliate because it sees the Human Rights Watch/Asia report as a biased and anti-Chinese document and thus will reduce the number of children it allows to leave for adoption in the West. But we believe this will not be the case. The PRC may temporarily react by reducing the number of orphans it allows to leave the country, but in all likelihood it will not dramatically curtail foreign adoption. In our opinion, 1999–2000 will see U.S. families continuing to adopt Chinese orphans in numbers similar to previous years.

What is at stake is a vast pool of legally free-for-adoption female orphans—enough, one might estimate, to satisfy much of the Western world's demand for children. Some observers guess that the orphans who reside in the approximately seventy orphanages throughout China number in the hundreds of thousands. Although the PRC admits to having about 100,000 children in orphanages, the United Nations puts the figure at 50,000 for only one province.[30] In fact, it is estimated that about 150,000 girls are abandoned every year, not counting the unknown number who are drowned.[31]

In sum, the PRC provides a quick and efficient adoption process, and, more important for many older (and single) potential U.S. adopters, the age eligibility of adopters is higher than that allowed by U.S. agencies. The same holds for PRC citizens. As of April 1999, China lowered the minimum age for foreign and Chinese adoptive parents to thirty, down from thirty-five.[32] Significantly, the new law will also allow Chinese citizens to adopt a second child. This is not a harbinger that Chinese authorities are abandoning their "one child policy": rather, that in certain areas, they are relaxing enforcement.

The controversy over the Human Rights Watch report demonstrates once again the tenuous reliability of any one country as a source of adoptable children in the West. Whether problems arise from (1) allegations of child kidnapping in Paraguay and Brazil, (2) accusations of the duping of young Central American peasant women for their infants, (3) charges that children sent to the West for adoption were actually being sent for their body parts, or (4) claims that female intercountry adoptees were being sold into prostitution, ICA has always been vulnerable to the winds of rumor, suspicion or arbitrary suspension, reduction or elimination on the part of the supplying country. Although in 1999 China is America's main provider of children, diplomatic relations between the two countries have at times been strained. The consequence of any political row could be the reduction or curtailment of the flow of children to the United States.

Vietnam

After the United States withdrew its forces from South Vietnam, the North Vietnamese quickly halted the policy of allowing Vietnamese children to be adopted by foreigners, especially Americans. In 1975, while Vietnam was ruled by a government friendly to the United States, 655 Vietnamese children were adopted by Americans. In 1980, practically no Vietnamese children were available for international adoption. The easing of tensions between the United States and the new government in Hanoi led to an increase in the number of children who were allowed to leave Vietnam for adoption by American families. Intercountry adoption from Vietnam jumped from 12 children in 1989 (table 1.4) to 603 by 1998.

Relative to either Korea or the PRC, intercountry adoption from Vietnam is infrequent and we think will remain so. But if Vietnam consistently allows about 500 to 600 of its children to be adopted by U.S. citizens, it will exceed the Philippines and India in the number of orphans who are allowed to be adopted by Americans. For years the

Table 1.4 Selected Asian Countries, 1989–1998

Year	Asia	Japan	India	Philippines	Thailand	Vietnam	Other Asian*	Total All Regions
1989	5,112	74	677	481	99	12	75	7,948
1990	3,823	60	361	423	111	53	65	7,088
1991	3,194	83	448	417	127	17	69	9,008
1992	3,032	71	348	353	90	23	81	6,536
1993	3,163	59	342	358	65	105	80	7,348
1994	3,687	51	390	320	45	288	84	8,200
1995	4,843	61	368	293	50	316	77	9,384
1996	6,100	38	381	228	53	354	73	11,316
1997	6,483	45	349	163	63	425	81	13,621
1998	7,827	39	478	200	84	603	82	15,774

Source: U.S. Department of State and Immigration and Naturalization Service. Reported in "The Bulletin of the Joint Council on International Children's Services" (Spring 1999); and *http://www.travel.state.gov/orphan_html* "Immigrant Visas Issued to Orphans Coming to U.S."
*Cambodia, others

Philippines and India have been relatively reliable sources of adoptable children.

In summary, while Asia remains the prime source of adoptees for American families, the relationship between sending and receiving countries is, as we have suggested, always uncomfortable, particularly from the perspective of the supplying country. Asia's reliability as a permanent source of adoptable children is therefore questionable and volatile, in spite of the recent media attention given to the availability of Chinese orphans. We do not believe that Chinese authorities will open the flood gates to intercountry adoption. They will not become another Korea.

Tables 1.3 and 1.4 demonstrate the relative consistency of ICAs from Asia. Although there are fluctuations within each country by year, the single factor influencing Asia's overall totals is the number of children Korea has allowed to leave the country.

Latin American ICA

From 1989 through 1998 the countries of Latin America (Central and South America) accounted for about 13 percent of all intercountry adoptees entering the United States. The data in tables 1.5 and 1.6 provide a breakdown for selected Central and South American countries from 1989 to 1998.

From 1989 to 1998, Colombia allowed the largest number of its orphans to be sent to the United States, representing about one-third of all Latin American ICAs. Note that in 1989 Peru allowed 269 of its children to be adopted by Americans. Two years later, that figure jumped to 722, or 37 percent of all South American adoptions. Six years after that, in 1997, Peru was not among the top twenty countries, allowing only 14 of its Peruvian-born orphans to be adopted by U.S. families.

Similarly, in Central America, two leading suppliers of orphans to U.S. families, El Salvador and Honduras, dramatically reduced the number of orphans they allowed to leave for the United States after 1992 and even more dramatically after 1993. In 1992 the number of orphans sent to the United States from El Salvador was 115 and from Honduras, 253. By 1998 those figures fell to 13 and 7, respectively. Guatemala, on the other hand, increased the number of children it allowed to be adopted in the United States from 208 in 1989 to 911 in 1998.

But El Salvador is a special case that warrants a brief explanation.

Table 1.5   Total from South America, 1989–1998

Year	Brazil	Chile	Colombia	Ecuador	Paraguay	Peru	Bolivia	Other (SA)	South America (SA)	Total All Regions
1989	180	254	735	19	254	269	28	18	1,757	7,948
1990	231	300	628	20	285	441	29	23	1,957	7,088
1991	178	263	527	11	177	722	51	20	1,949	9,008
1992	139	176	403	36	244	324	74	22	1,418	6,536
1993	178	61	416	42	405	2	123	16	1,471	7,348
1994	150	77	342	42	497	37	42	18	1,205	8,200
1995	134	86	338	70	332[a]	15	21	8	1,004	9,384
1996	101	62	258	52	261	17	35	19	805	11,316
1997	91	41	233	43	13	14	77	16	548	13,621
1998	103	26	351	55	7	26	73	14	655	15,774

Source: U.S. Department of State and Immigration and Naturalization Service. Reported in the "Bulletin of the Joint Council on International Children's Services" (Spring 1999); and *http://www.travel.state.gov/orphan_html* "Immigrant Visas Issued to Orphans Coming to U.S."
[a]The *New York Times* reports this figure to be 410 children. ("Adoptions in Paraguay: Mothers Cry Theft," Diana Jean Schemo, *NYT,* March 19, 1996, p. 1.)

Table 1.6   Totals from Mexico, Caribbean, and Selected Central American Countries, 1989–1998

Year	Mexico	Caribbean*	El Salvador	Costa Rica	Guatemala	Honduras	Total	Total All Regions
1989	107	202	92	78	208	191	878	7,948
1990	123	158	105	107	263	203	959	7,088
1991	106	159	122	55	324	244	1,010	9,008
1992	104	134	115	65	428	253	1,099	6,536
1993	97	150	97	48	512	183	1,087	7,348
1994	95	130	39	28	431	76	799	8,200
1995	91	115	30	19	436	27	718	9,384
1996	89	135	19	20	420	28	711	11,316
1997	152	200	5	22	788	26	1,193	13,621
1998	168	314	13	7	911	7	1,420	15,774

Source: U.S. Department of State and Immigration and Naturalization Service. Reported in "The Bulletin of the Joint Council on International Children's Services" (Spring 1999); and http://www.travel.state.gov/orphan_html "Immigrant Visas Issued to Orphans Coming to U.S."
 *Dominican Republic, Haiti, Jamaica, other Caribbean islands.

From 1979 to 1991 a bloody civil war raged, killing some 75,000 out of its population of five million. Not only were many children killed and wounded during this conflict, but an unknown number were stolen from their parents to be adopted domestically and internationally. Some children found their way to the United States (many Guatemalan children were also stolen from their parents during its thirty-six-year civil war). Curiously, no pre-adoption investigations were done by U.S. authorities in El Salvador prior to the late 1980s, allowing untold numbers of children to be adopted by U.S. citizens, many no doubt illegally.[33] An organization known as Pro-Busqueda (Search) is now investigating several U.S. adoptions and questioning their legality. Naturally, the proverbial knock on the door by an organization like Pro-Busqueda is an adoptive parent's worst nightmare, causing considerable consternation among the community of American families who adopted children born in El Salvador.

Europe

Only recently has Europe become a major presence in intercountry adoption. In 1989 just 120 orphans were adopted by parents in the

United States; ten years later the number had increased to 5,660. In 1991 Europe surpassed Latin America by a factor of almost three in the number of intercountry adoptees allowed to leave for the United States. As table 1.7 shows, 2,552 of the 2,761 European children adopted in 1991 by American parents were Romanian. From 1993 through 1998, most of the children were adopted from Russia.

In 1991 the plight of Romania's orphans and orphanages made front-page news in most of the world's press. Prior to the breakup of Soviet-dominated Eastern Europe, the Romanian government mandated that women procreate. Failure to have children meant in many cases loss of job, housing, medical coverage, and so on. In fact, women were encouraged to have children with the clear promise that the state would provide for their children. One result of this draconian policy was that thousands of children were placed in state-operated orphanages because their families were unable economically and/or emotionally to support them. But the orphanages and necessary professional care

Table 1.7 Total from Europe, 1989–1998

Year	Romania	Russian Federation	Poland	Ukraine	Bulgaria	Other European*	All Europe	Total All Regions
1989	2		68		1	49	120	7,948
1990	90		67		3	72	232	7,088
1991	2,552		95		8	106	2,761	9,008
1992	145	314	109	48	90	168	874	6,536
1993	88	695	70	248	126	294	1,521	7,348
1994	197†	1,324	100	163	101	485	2,370	8,200
1995	260	1,684	32	5	108	571	2,660	9,384
1996	554	2,328	66	10	157	453	3,568	11,316
1997	621	3,816	78	59	148	454	5,176	13,621
1998	406	4,491	77	180	151	355	5,660	15,774

Source: U.S. Department of State and Immigration and Naturalization Service. Reported in "The Bulletin of the Joint Council on International Children's Services" (Spring 1999); and *http://www.travel.state.gov/orphan_html* "Immigrant Visas Issued to Orphans Coming to U.S."
*Belarus, Georgia, Hungary, Kazakhatan, Latvia, Lithuania, Moldova, other
†The *New York Times* reports that in 1995, 269 Romanian orphans were adopted by U.S. citizens. In 1994, reports that figure to be 249 children. ("Romanian 'Orphans': Prisoners of Their Cribs," Jane Perlez, *NYT,* March 25, 1996, p. 1.)

could not keep pace with Romania's population growth. Intercountry adoption was seen as one way of dealing with this unprecedented increase of children without parents. It led to a child welfare system out of control, not reined in until 1991–1992. The conditions in Romania's orphanages were described as appalling. Allegations were made of official corruption. Descriptions were rampant of children being fraudulently removed from their birth mothers and sent to the West. To curb the seemingly uncontrolled flow of children from Romania to the West, the government terminated practically all intercountry adoptions and created the Romanian Adoption Committee (RAC). In 1992 and 1993 Howard Altstein was a consultant to the RAC in Bucharest. Composed of dedicated and concerned individuals, the RAC was empowered by the government to examine the issue of parentless children and design new adoption strategies. A series of meetings was held in Romania with the RAC and recommendations were forwarded to responsible authorities. Although we cannot establish a direct link between the recommendations and actions taken subsequently by the Romanian government, the number of children allowed to leave Romania for adoption in the West plunged from 1992 onward. In 1998 only 406 Romanian orphans were adopted in the United States.

Yet Romania's orphanages remain full. Romanian authorities say that in 1994 their orphanages held 104,000 children, up from 80,000 children the previous year.[34] But in an unknown number of cases, many (some say most) of these children are not orphans as we recognize the term. In other words, their parents have not voluntarily relinquished parental rights, nor have the courts terminated parental rights. Many of these children remain in limbo due almost exclusively to economic factors. Parents, usually mothers, place their infants in orphanages because they are unable to provide for them. Mothers tell orphanage directors that their children's stay will be temporary until the families' economic condition improves. But in the overwhelming number of cases this never occurs, and the children remain in an orphanage. The children are neither legally declared orphans nor able to return home. As of this writing, despite the number of children in its orphanages, Romania resembles the rest of Europe in allowing few children to leave for adoption.

Intercountry adoption of Russian children remains problematic. Once a world power influential in setting a global agenda, Russia now is seemingly unable to care for its own orphaned children. To lessen its embarrassment and to thwart the flow of children to the West, Russia enacted legislation in 1994 mandating thorough searches for in-country adopters before orphaned children may be considered candidates for intercountry adoption. Many observers attribute this statute, and Romania's law that was passed several years earlier, as being based for the most part on national pride. They are laws that are intentionally promulgated to slow the flow of Russian and Romanian orphans to the West.[35] In 1993 American families adopted 695 orphans from the Russian Federation. In 1994 another 1,324 Russian children were adopted by Americans.[36] Of course, unknown additional numbers were adopted in other Western countries.

Yet as if to offset the 1994 ruling, in March 1995 President Yeltsin signed a new adoption law making all Russian orphans eligible for international adoptions, not just the physically disabled or children of alcoholic or mentally ill parents. But in line with the 1994 statute, the law requires an initial search for Russian adoptive parents.[37] Nevertheless, in 1998 Russia allowed 4,491 of its children to be adopted in the United States, more than in any other year and more than any other country, including China.

It is particularly difficult to predict future intercountry adoption trends from Eastern Europe. Countries such as Poland, the Ukraine, and the Baltic Republics have major economic problems and enormous economic potential. Although they do allow small numbers of orphans to be adopted in the United States, they will not easily relinquish their orphans to the West on a sustained basis.

SUMMARY

In 1998 two-thirds of all foreign-born adoptees came from three countries: Russia, China, and South Korea. One might say that this is no different than it ever was when (in 1989) South Korea alone provided almost half of all foreign-born children adopted by U.S. families. But

Table 1.8   Number of Intercountry Adoptions, Selected Countries, 1989 and 1998

Country	1989	1998
China	142	4,263
Korea	3,552	1,829
Romania	2	406
Guatemala	208	911
India	677	478
Vietnam	12	603
Russian Federation	0	4,491
Paraguay	254	7
Colombia	735	351
Philippines	481	200
Ukraine	0	180
Bulgaria	1	151
Caribbean	202	314
Brazil	180	103
Mexico	107	168

in 1998 each of the three largest suppliers of children to the United States were and continue to be problematic for different reasons. Russia appears to be tottering on the brink of implosion, with unknown consequences. Relations with China, for the most part, always seem tenuous. South Korea is on public record as working toward the elimination of all intercountry adoption from its country.

Having said this, we also recognize that the pattern for intercountry adoptions seems to be that as one source of adoptable children diminishes, other countries increase the number of children they allow to be adopted abroad or else new sources appear. For example, it was not until 1993 that Russia permitted 695 children to be adopted by Americans. The following year that number doubled, to 1,324 children. By 1998 Russia was the largest supplier of foreign-born orphans to U.S. families (4,491 children). Until 1992 the number of orphans who had been allowed to leave Russia for the United States was zero.

In 1992 Vietnam allowed 23 of its children to be adopted in the United States. In 1998 that number was 603. Guatemala allowed U.S.

families to adopt 1,420 of its children in 1996. By 1998 it allowed 911 children to leave for the United States.

What these numbers reveal are the vagaries of intercountry adoption. Countries that for many years allowed their children to be adopted abroad have, without explanation, reduced, eliminated, or increased the number of orphans they now allow to leave the country. Internal political, economic, and social stability plays heavily on a country's behavior vis-à-vis international adoption. Whereas one day Western eyes are focused on the countries of Eastern Europe (especially Russia) as potential sources of adoptable children, the next day they are focused on adoption opportunities in China or Paraguay. Although India and the Philippines remain relatively stable in the number of children they allow to leave their country, the Central American states appear volatile. This ever-changing world situation leaves potential adopters, not just those in the United States, scurrying around the globe for children. As the twentieth century comes to a close, it is reported that the Marshall Islands will begin and Ethiopia will expand their programs in intercountry adoption.[38]

You may wonder, why do we compare the experiences of transracially and intercountry adoptees? One group is grounded in the American experience, whereas the other is foreign-born and has no ties to the United States. Our answer is that these groups share many important characteristics. Most of them are members of a racial minority group. All have been raised in multiracial environments with white parents and, in many cases, white siblings. In some instances they were raised with other racially and ethnically different adopted siblings. These shared characteristics make the transracial and intercountry adoptees uniquely comparable.

NOTES

1. Elizabeth Shepherd, "Adopting Negro Children: White Families Find It Can Be Done," *New Republic* (June 20, 1964): 10–12; Harriet Fricke, "Interracial Adoption: The Little Revolution," *Social Work*, vol. 10, no. 3 (July 1965): 92–97.

2. Bernice Madison and Michael Shapiro, "Black Adoption-Issues and Policies," *Social Service Review*, vol. 47, no. 4, (December 1973): 531–554.

3. "Opportunity: Survey of Adoption of Black Children" (Portland, Oreg.: Boys and Girls Aid Society of Oregon, 1969–1976).

4. Child Welfare League of America, *Standards for Adoption Practice* (New York: CWLA, 1968).

5. Child Welfare League of America, *Standards for Adoption Practice* (New York: CWLA, 1973).

6. For a fuller description of the TRA movement, see Rita J. Simon and Howard Altstein, *Adoption, Race and Identity* (New York: Praeger, 1992), chap. 1.

7. Child Welfare League of America, *Standards for Adoption Service*, rev. ed. (New York: CWLA, 1988), p. 34.

8. Ibid., p. 35.

9. Henry Maas, "The Successful Adoptive Parent Application," *Social Work*, vol. 5, no. 1 (January 1960): 14–20; Helen Fradkin, "Adoptive Parents for Children with Special Needs," *Child Welfare*, vol. 37, no. 1 (January 1958): 1–6. Michael Shapiro, "A Study of Adoption Practice," vol. 1: *Adoption Agencies and the Children They Serve* (New York: Child Welfare League of America, 1956), pp. 75, 80–83; Child Welfare League of America, *Standards for Adoption Service* (New York: CWLA, 1958), p. 25, section 4.9, ibid., footnote, pp. 76–86; Florence G. Brown, "What Do We Seek in Adoptive Parents?," *Social Casework*, vol. 32, no. 4 (1951): 155–161, Child Welfare League of America, op. cit., footnote 27, pp. 75, 87; ibid., pp. 75–76.

10. North American Council on Adoptable Children, "Barriers to Same Race Placement" (St. Paul, Minn.: North American Council on Adoptable Children, 1991).

11. "The Orphanage Option," editorial, *Washington Post*, April 24, 1994, p. PC6, and Ellen Goodman, "Who Has the Rights to Black Children?," *Baltimore Sun*, December 7, 1993, p. 19A.

12. Packard Foundation, "The Future of Children," *Adoption*, vol. 3, no. 1 (Spring 1993): 63.

13. Ibid.: 63.

14. Op. cit., no. 13: 29.

15. Op. cit., no. 13: 34.

16. Op. cit., no. 13: 34.

17. Bachrach, Christine A.; Adams, Patricia F.; Sambrano, Soledad; London, Kathryn A. "Adoption in the 1980s," *Advance Data from Vital and Health Statistics*, no. 181 (Hyattsville, Md.: National Center for Health Statistics, 1989).

18. Chun, B. H., "Adoption and Korea," *Child Welfare*, vol. 58, no. 2 (April 1989): 255–260.

19. Peter Maass, "Orphans: Korea's Disquieting Problem," *Washington Post,* December 12, 1988, p. 1.

20. "Immigrant Visas Issued to Orphans Coming to U.S." <http://www.travel.state.gov/orphan_html>

21. National Broadcasting Corporation, 10:45 P.M., September 19, 1988; Maass, p. 1; Tamar Lewin, "South Korea Slows Export of Babies for Adoption," *New York Times,* February 12, 1990, p. B10.

22. Bruce Porter, "I Met My Daughter at the Wuhan Founding Hospital," *New York Times Magazine,* April 11, 1993, p. 24.

23. "South Korea to Restrict Adoptions by Foreigners," no author, *Baltimore Sun,* December 26, 1993, p. 16.

24. Elisabeth Rosenthal, "For One-Child Policy, China Rethinks Iron Hand," *New York Times,* November 1, 1998, p. 1.

25. Elaine Louie, "Now Chosen, Chinese Girls Take to the U.S.," *New York Times,* April 27, 1995, p. C11.

26. Reuters, "China Detains Official Linked to Orphanage Abuse Report," *Baltimore Sun,* January 24, 1996, p. 14a.

27. Holly Burkhalter, "China's Horrific Adoption Mills," *New York Times,* January 11, 1996, p. 25.

28. Felicia R. Lee, "Anxious Vigils for Chinese Babies," *New York Times,* January 18, 1996, p. C.1.

29. Ibid.

30. Op. cit., no. 27.

31. Steve Mills, "Americans Rush to Adopt Rejected Chinese Girls," *Baltimore Sun,* May 21, 1995, p. 2A.

32. Joint Council on International Children's Services, Cheverly, MD 20785, 301-229-8300.

33. Tina Rosenberg, "What Did You Do in the War, Mama?," *New York Times Magazine,* Feb. 7, 1999, p. 52.

34. Jane Perlez, "Romanian 'Orphans': Prisoners of Their Cribs," *New York Times,* March 25, 1996, p. 1.

35. Alessandra Stanley, "Nationalism Slows Foreign Adoptions in Russia," *New York Times,* December 12, 1994, p. 1.

36. Ibid.

37. "Russia Eases Rules on Foreign Adoption," no author, *Baltimore Sun,* March 8, 1995, p. 12.

38. Joint Council on International Children's Services, Cheverly, MD 20785, 301-229-8300.

2

+

The Legal Perspective on Transracial and Intercountry Adoptions

Adoption is a legal process in which a child's legal rights and duties toward his natural parents, and vice versa, are terminated and similar rights and duties are created with respect to the child's adoptive parents. Unknown in common law, adoption was first created in the United States through an 1851 Massachusetts statute. By 1931 every state in the union had passed adoption statutes.

Adoption, like other family law issues, is the province of the states. Therefore, the law of the state in which the adoption is to take place will control the arrangements. The legal structure for adoption consists of the adoption statutes, the case law interpreting those statutes, and—perhaps most important—the placement practices of the public and private adoption agencies whose role it is to provide services to parents who wish to place children for adoption and to choose adoptive homes for them. The objective of this legal structure is to seek adoptions that serve the best interest of the child.

THE ROLE OF RACE IN ADOPTION CASES

Since the 1940s, race has been treated by the U.S. Supreme Court as a "suspect classification" under the Equal Protection clause of the federal Constitution. This means that the use of race in an official decision is subject to strict judicial scrutiny. Racial classifications are valid only when they are justified by a compelling governmental interest and are necessary to the accomplishment of that legitimate state purpose. In 1967 the Court—relying on other cases that applied strict scrutiny analysis—struck down laws prohibiting racial intermarriage, in *Loving v. Virginia.*[1] After that, state laws prohibiting transracial adoption were either repealed by state legislatures or held unconstitutional. In *In re Gomez,*[2] the Texas Court of Appeals reached the conclusion that the law prohibiting transracial adoption violated the federal and Texas constitutions. In *Compos v. McKeithen,*[3] the federal district court for Louisiana held unconstitutional a Louisiana statute that limited adoptions to children belonging to the same race as the adopter. In 1984 the U.S. Supreme Court looked at a closely related issue: the use of race in a custody decision between divorced parents. In *Palmore v. Sidoti,*[4] a white couple had been divorced and the mother awarded custody of their child. When the mother married a black man, the father sought to gain custody of the child. The trial judge granted the change, saying:

> This court feels that despite the strides that have been made in bettering relations between the races in this country, it is inevitable that Melanie will, if allowed to remain in her present situation and attain school age and thus be more vulnerable to peer pressures, suffer from the social stigmatization that is sure to come.[5]

The U.S. Supreme Court reversed the decision, acknowledging that the child's welfare was the controlling factor but finding that the Florida court had based its decision solely on race: "It is clear that the outcome would have been different had [the mother] married a Caucasian male of similar respectability." The U.S. Supreme Court recognized that the Florida court was correct in saying that racial prejudice exists and that "there is a risk that a child living with a stepparent of a different race may be subject to a variety of pressures and stresses not present if the child were living with parents of the same racial or ethnic origin." But the Supreme Court held that "the effects of prejudice, however real, cannot justify a racial classification removing an infant child from the custody of its natural mother found to be an appropriate person to have such custody."

Palmore v. Sidoti involved a custody dispute between the child's natural parents; therefore, the relevance of this precedent for transracial adoption may be limited. However, the issues are closely enough related that *Palmore* ought not be ignored when considering how the Court might apply the Fourteenth Amendment to an adoption case. Particularly important is the fact that racial considerations did not control the court's consideration of the child's best interests.

Prior to the U.S. Supreme Court ruling in *Loving v. Virginia*, which clearly foreshadowed the demise of prohibitions on interracial adoptions, courts followed a general rule when deciding on the role that race should play in adoption decisions: Race may be considered in determining the best interest of the child, but it cannot be controlling.

That rule continued to be the approach of the courts. For example, in *Compos*—the case striking down the Louisiana statute prohibiting transracial adoptions—the court noted that, although recognition of the difficulties of interracial adoption could not justify race as the deciding factor in an adoption, it did justify consideration of race as a relevant factor.

Often the courts do not analyze why race can constitutionally be considered on the issue of the best interests of the child. Based on precedent—that is, the holdings of prior cases—courts assume that the constitutional issue is whether race is the sole determining consideration or only one of the relevant factors. In *Drummond v. Fulton County Department of Family and Children's Services*,[6] the U.S. Court of Appeals for the Fifth Circuit was faced with white foster parents alleging that the denial of their petition to adopt their black foster child was based solely on race and that this violated their right to equal protection. The district court had found that the petition was denied solely on the basis of race. The court of appeals did not disturb this finding. However, it recognized that the decision makers had definitely taken the race of the parties into account. Thus, the specific issue was whether this limited use of race was valid. The court concluded that considering race as a factor was constitutionally permissible. It noted that "no case has been cited to the court suggesting that it is impermissible to consider race in adoption placement. The only cases which have addressed this problem indicate that, while the automatic use of race is barred, the use of race as one of the factors in making the ultimate decision is legitimate."

One court even stated that failure to consider race as one of the relevant factors is an error. The case in which the court took that position was *In re Davis.*[7] The court was faced with competing claims for custody from a black couple with whom two siblings of the child had been placed and an elderly white couple who had raised and cared for the black child from three days after his birth until the age of four. The elderly white couple had been denied custody and sought review of the decision. One of the grounds of error they claimed was that the lower court had neglected to consider race as a factor in the decision. The Pennsylvania Supreme Court agreed that a failure to consider race in adoption proceedings was erroneous, but that in the circumstances of this case the error was harmless, as the racial factor would have worked *against* the white couple anyway. In the process of discussing the place of race in adoption decisions, the court said that "critical commentary, as well as near unanimous precedent, overwhelmingly adopt the position that the respective races of the participants is a *factor* to be considered in a child's placement determination but, *as with all factors, can be no more than that—a factor.*"[8] In a few cases, the courts have applied standard Fourteenth Amendment Equal Protection analysis and subjected the use of race in the adoption decision to strict scrutiny. Even under that analysis, the courts have found that consideration of race in an adoption is constitutionally acceptable. In *Petition of R.M.G.,*[9] for example, the District of Columbia Court of Appeals—applying strict scrutiny to the District adoption statute—found that the best interest of the child was a compelling state interest and that the race of the child and the adoptive parents was relevant to that compelling state interest. It reasoned that because adoptees often have difficulty with a sense of identity, and because the attitude of the parents toward race—in transracial adoptions—may be highly relevant to the child's sense of identity, those responsible for an adoption decision "will not be able to focus adequately on an adoptive child's sense of identity, and thus on the child's best interest, without considering race."

The court concluded, "In sum, an inherently suspect, indeed presumptively invalid, racial classification in the adoption statute is, in a constitutional sense, necessary to advance a compelling governmental interest: the best interest of the child. It thus survives strict scrutiny—a result that is unusual, as racial classifications go, but not precluded."

In *McLaughlin v. Pernsley*,[10] the court granted a preliminary injunction to white foster parents whose black foster child had been removed from their care solely on the basis of race, requiring the City of Philadelphia to return the child. The court found that the goal of providing for the child's racial and cultural needs in order to effect the best interests of the child was a compelling governmental interest for the purposes of the Equal Protection clause. However, the court then found that the use of race as the sole criterion for a placement was not necessary to accomplish that compelling state interest. The court held that the decision to remove the black child from the white foster home violated the Equal Protection Rights of the black child and the white foster parents.

Another view of the basic rules governing the use of race in adoptions was expressed by the District of Columbia Court of Appeals in *Petition of D.I.S.*[11] It held that Equal Protection analysis does not require that strict scrutiny be applied to the use of race in adoption decisions. The District adoption statute, said the court, only requires that information on the race of the petitioner and the child be included in the adoption petition and does not therefore require that the court give it any consideration. Because the statute does not separate persons solely on the basis of racial classification or give preference for that reason, it was not subject to strict scrutiny.

FEDERAL LEGISLATION

The Indian Child Welfare Act

The Indian Child Welfare Act of 1978 virtually prohibits the adoption of Indian children by non-Indians. This legislation was enacted by Congress under its authority over American-Indian affairs and governs the adoption of Indian children.[12] The most important feature of the Indian Child Welfare Act is that it gives the tribal courts exclusive jurisdiction over child custody proceedings involving children who reside or are domiciled on the reservation, as well as concurrent but presumptive tribal jurisdiction over an American-Indian child not domiciled on the reservation. The act also contains provisions governing proceedings that take place in state courts. Of these, the most important substantive provision relates to adoptive placements under state law and the provision mandates:

> In any adoptive placement of an Indian child under state law, a preference shall be given, in the absence of a good cause to the contrary, to a placement with (a) a member of the child's extended family; (b) other members of the Indian child's tribe; or (c) other Indian families.[13]

In *Mississippi Band of Choctaw Indians v. Holyfield*,[14] the U.S. Supreme Court discussed the Indian Child Welfare Act in the context of holding void the adoption of an Indian child by non-Indian parents in a Mississippi state court. The Supreme Court held that the Mississippi court's decree was void for lack of jurisdiction. It found that the act displaced state court jurisdiction in favor of tribal courts even in a case like *Holyfield*, where an Indian mother who was domiciled on the reservation gave birth to a child off the reservation, because the domicile of the child follows that of the mother. The Supreme Court recognized that this result protected tribal authority over children born to reservation domiciliaries even where the child's parents sought to avoid tribal authority and to place the child for adoption with a non-Indian couple. The Court found that Congress intended to protect tribal sovereignty over individual Indian choices, quoting the American Indian Policy Review Commission that "removal of Indian children from their cultural setting seriously impacts long-term tribal survival." This objective of preserving Indian tribes is the justification for the role that race plays in the Indian Child Welfare Act.

The 1994 and 1997 Federal Statutes

Prior to the passage by the United States Congress in 1994 of the Multi-Ethnic Placement Act (MEPA)[15] and in 1997 of the Adoption and Safe Families Act,[16] transracial adoptions were governed by the same

laws as other adoptions.[17] The purpose of both these acts was to prohibit the use of race "to delay or deny the placement of a child for
adoption or foster care on the basis of race, color, or national origin of
the adoptive or foster parent or child involved."

While the main supporters of the 1994 act had the previous objec-
tives as their goals, the act also contained the following language:

> An agency may consider the cultural, ethnic, or racial background of the
> child and the capacity of the prospective foster or adoptive parents to
> meet the needs of the child of this background as one of a number of
> factors used to determine the best interests of the child.[18]

This paragraph thwarted the original intention of the act to remove
race as a consideration and, in fact, freed agencies and states to continue to consider a child's racial background in determining placement. It took three more years until the 1997 act was passed that
clearly prohibited the use of race to delay or deny placements.

States found to be in violation would have their quarterly federal
funds reduced by 2 percent for the first violation, by 5 percent for the
second violation, and by 10 percent for the third or subsequent viola-
tions. Private entities that are found to be in violation for one quarter
would be required to return to the secretary all federal funds received
from the state during the quarter. In addition, any individual who is
harmed by a violation of this provision may seek redress in any
United States district court.

Prior to the intervention of the federal government in 1994 and 1997,
twenty states included race as a consideration in the adoption process.
Ten of those states simply stated that the race of one or more of the
parties directly affected by the adoption was to be included in the petition for adoption. But their statutes were silent as to how the information should be used by those in a position to make final decisions
concerning adoption. Arkansas and Minnesota had laws that specifically required that preference be given to adoption within the same
racial group. New Jersey and California statutes provided that an
agency may not discriminate with regard to the selection of adoptive
parents on the basis of race but then provided that race might be considered in determining the best interests of the child. Kentucky stat-

utes claimed that agencies may not deny placement on the basis of race unless the biological parents express a clear desire to so discriminate, in which case their wishes must be respected.

At the time this book went to press, data just became available that will allow us to assess the effectiveness of the 1997 Adoption and Safe Families Act in moving minority children out of institutions and foster care and into adoptive homes. It is too early to determine whether the states have found ways to ignore the intent of the act and will continue to do business as usual. Empirically, answers to these questions are of great importance, but, unfortunately, they must await the results of surveys and other efforts that are currently being made to determine what is actually happening.

INTERCOUNTRY ADOPTION

An intercountry adoption—that is, the adoption of a child who is a resident of a foreign country by U.S. parents—requires compliance with three sets of rules:

(1) The law of the country of the child's birth. In current adoption practice, this country—which is usually an economically struggling Third World country—is often called either the "sending country," because it sends its children to other (richer) countries for adoption, or the "country of origin," because the children are from that country.

(2) The regulations of the Immigration and Naturalization Service (INS), which must be followed so the child will be admitted to the United States.

(3) The laws of the state where the adoptive parents live.

Each of these aspects of the legal framework for intercountry adoption is described further on.

In order to prevent tragic adoption challenges by putative parents (in most cases, fathers) that they were not consulted in the adoption of their children to U.S. nationals, the INS implemented a law on October 1, 1994, requiring that both birth parents approve of their child's being adopted in the United States. The American statute assumes all births are legitimate, thereby requiring the authorization of both parents to allow their child to leave his or her birth country to be adopted in the United States. The law was enacted with all good intentions, to prevent one of the birth parents (in most cases, the birth father) from challenging the legitimacy of the foreign adoption after the child had been sent abroad, on the grounds that he or she was not consulted about the child's adoption.

But the new statute poses several difficulties for American adopters. For example, many birth mothers who relinquish their children for foreign adoption either do not know who the father was or, among those who know his identity, do not know his whereabouts. Proof must be furnished of a putative father's death or of his abandonment of his family. The law defines a two-year desertion as proof of abandonment. Second, several countries, especially Romania and those in Latin America, do not distinguish between a legitimate birth (a child born to a married couple) and an illegitimate birth (a child born to an unwed mother), but the United States, as noted previously, assumes all births to be legitimate, requiring the approval of both parents. Past U.S. law required the approval of only one parent.

THE LAW OF THE CHILD'S RESIDENCE

Most sending countries in international adoptions require that the child be adopted in that country. A few allow proxy adoptions, which enable parents to adopt without traveling to the county in which the child resides. Others allow the child to leave the sending country to be adopted in the United States. If the country requires that the child be adopted in his or her country of origin, an international adoption requires that one or both of the prospective parents travel to the sending country and remain there long enough to process the adoption. This can be a long, frustrating, and expensive process.[19] The requirement that an adoption be made in the country of residence is regarded as one of the main problems in intercountry adoptions.

As part of the adoption process, a home study conducted in the United States by an authorized agency is required. The country of the child's residence may also require that a local "home study" be conducted in that country.

After the requirements of the sending country are met, either through adoption or clearance for placement in the United States, a passport for the child must be obtained from the sending country to enable the child to travel to the United States.

U.S. IMMIGRATION LAWS

In order for a foreign adoption to be recognized for immigration into the United States, three requirements must be fulfilled.[20] First, the state law where the adoptive parents reside must be satisfied, as must the law of the sending country of the child's origin. Second, the parents must be considered suitable to adopt, as shown by a home study conducted by an agency approved in the United States. And third, the child must satisfy the U.S. immigration law definition of "orphan." This stringent definition frequently causes problems because it may not include all of the children who are legally free for adoption in the foreign country. Persons knowledgeable about intercountry adoption warn that there is a real danger that foreign agencies and intermediaries not fully knowledgeable about U.S. immigration law may process the adoptions of children who are legally free for adoption in the foreign country but who do not meet the U.S. definition of "orphan."

THE HAGUE CONFERENCE ON PRIVATE
INTERNATIONAL LAW

Not without some controversy is the Hague Convention on Protection of Children and Cooperation in Respect of Intercountry Adoption (THC). Recommended by the Hague Convention on Private International Law, a private nongovernmental entity whose mission is to institute and oversee treaties, THC was convened to examine various ways that countries process intercountry adoption and then recommend minimum uniform procedures to be followed by all signatories of THC.[21] Its goals "are to set minimum standards for intercountry adoption that will allow recognition of adoption among the party countries, protect the interests of the children, birth parents, and adoptive parents, and prevent illegal child trafficking."[22]

As of September 1998, the United States and some thirty-three other countries are signatories to the Hague Convention.[23] The convention on Intercountry Adoptions was sent to the Senate in June 1998 for ratification. Being a signatory only represents intent to go further with the ratification process.

Thirty countries ratified/acceded to THC.[24] The United States is not one of them. Even if the United States does ratify THC, most agree that ratification will not fundamentally change the way American families go about adopting foreign-born children.[25] For the United States, THC has several problems. One is congressional speed. Since THC would be considered a treaty, it requires the advice and consent of the Senate, implementing legislation by the Congress, and the signature of the president. All this takes time. Some members of the adoption community are apprehensive that countries that have approved the treaty will only allow their children to be adopted by Western "receiving" countries who have likewise approved the treaty. This would exclude the United States until the treaty receives legislative sanction and is signed by the president.

But the biggest stumbling block to America's support of THC may not be congressional speed. As called for in THC, it is the need to establish a "central authority" to oversee the treaty's implementation. This would no doubt require Washington to either establish a new entity (e.g., within the Departments of State or Health and Human Services of the Immigration and Naturalization Service) to accomplish these tasks or give added responsibility to other sections within those departments. In either scenario, it would mean greater federal involvement into states' affairs at a time when the mantra of most legislators is "less government."

In any case, the United States must ratify and implement THC. Not doing so would leave countless American families with no source of adoptable children, since many American adoption agencies, in spite of the Adoption and Safe Families Act, continue to erect unlawful barriers that prevent American families from adopting racially different American children.

THE LAW OF THE ADOPTIVE PARENTS'
STATE OF RESIDENCE

The law of the adoptive parents' state of residence may require the adoptive parents to fulfill certain requirements, regardless of whether the adoption is processed in the foreign country. If the adoption was not finalized in the country, an adoption in the state of the adoptive parents' residence is required. This means complying with the adoption law of that state, which may require a period of residence with the adoptive family prior to finalization of the adoption.

If there was an adoption in the foreign country, it will usually be recognized by the U.S. courts; but adoptive parents are advised to have an adoption in the state of their residence as well, to ensure against legal problems that might arise. Also, it is useful to have local documents in English attesting to the birth and the adoption and to have those documents readily available for U.S. courts and agencies.[26]

NOTES

This chapter has been adapted from portions of chapter 2 of Rita J. Simon, Howard Altstein, and Marygold Melli, *The Case for Transracial Adoption* (Washington, D.C.: American University Press, 1994).

1. *Loving v. Virginia*, 388 U.S. 1 (1967).
2. *In re Gomez*, 424 S.W.2d 656 (Texas 1967).
3. *Compos v. McKeithen*, 341 F.Supp.264 (E.D.LA., 1972).
4. *Palmore v. Sidoti*, 466 U.S. 429 (1984).
5. Ibid., p. 433.
6. *Drummond v. Fulton County Department of Family and Children's Services*, 568 F.2d 1200 (5th Cir. 1977).
7. *In re Davis*, 465 A.2d 614 (Pa. 1983).
8. Ibid., at 622; emphasis in original.
9. *Petition of R.M.G.*, 454 A.2d 776 (D.C. App. 1982).
10. *McLaughlin v. Pernsley*, 693 F. Supp. 318 (E.D. Pa. 1988).
11. *Petition of D.I.S.*, 494 A.2d 1316 (D.C. App. 1985).
12. The Indian Child Welfare Act of 1978 is codified at 25 U.S.C., secs. 1901ff.
13. Ibid., sec. 1915(a).

14. *Mississippi Band of Choctaw Indians v. Holyfield,* 109 S.Ct.1597 (1989).

15. Multi-Ethnic Placement Act, 1994, P.L. 103–382.

16. Adoption and Safe Families Act, 1997, P.L. 105–89.

17. The Indian Child Welfare Act is specifically excluded from the 1994 and 1997 federal statutes.

18. Op. cit., P.L. 103–382.

19. See, for example, "Ordeal in Peru: Cuddling a Baby, Clinging to Hope," *New York Times,* June 9, 1992, p. A7.

20. Elizabeth Bartholet, "International Adoption Overview," in *Adoption Laws and Practices,* ed. J. Hollinger (New York: Matthew Bender, 1991), pp. 30–31.

21. The authors of this work are members of the Study Group on ICA of the Secretary of State's Advisory Committee on Private International Law.

22. "Status of U.S. Efforts to Ratify the Hague Adoption Convention," http://travelstate.gov/ratify.html

23. The Unites States signed in 1994.

24. Joint Council on International Children's Services, Cheverly, MD 20785, 301-229-8300.

25. "Intercountry Adoption: Procedures Are Reasonable, but Sometimes Inefficiently Administered," GAO/NSIAD-93-83, April 1993, p. 3.

26. Bartholet, op. cit., pp. 10–32.

3

✛

The Case against
Transracial Adoption

Organized opposition to transracial adoption, which began in the early part of the 1970s, was formidable enough by 1975 to bring about a reversal in policy by the leading adoption agencies in most states throughout the country. The opposition was led and organized primarily by the National Association of Black Social Workers (NABSW) and by leaders of black political organizations, who said they saw in the practice an insidious scheme for depriving the black community of its most valuable future resource: its children.

Opposition also came from some of the leaders of Native-American groups, who labeled transracial adoption "genocide" and who also accused white society of perpetuating its most malevolent scheme, that of seeking to deny Native Americans their future by taking away their children.

Both the black and Native-American groups who were opposed to transracial adoption agreed that it would be impossible for white parents to rear black or Indian children in an environment that would permit them to retain or develop a black or an Indian identity. Even if some white parents might want their adopted children to grow up Indian or black, they would lack the skills, insights, and experience necessary to foster this awareness in their children.

37

BLACK AMERICAN OPPOSITION

At its national conference in 1971, the president of the NABSW, William T. Merritt, said, "Black children should be placed only with Black families, whether in foster care or for adoption."[1] The following excerpt—beginning with this now well-known announcement—establishes the flavor of the speech.

> Black children should be placed only with Black families, whether in foster care or adoption. Black children belong physically, psychologically and culturally in Black families in order that they receive the total sense of themselves and develop a sound projection of their future. . . . Black children in white homes are cut off from the healthy development of themselves as Black people. The socialization process for every child begins at birth. Included in the socialization process is that child's cultural heritage which is an important segment of the total process. This must begin at the earliest moment; otherwise our children will not have the background and knowledge which is necessary to survive in a racist society. This is impossible if the child is placed with white parents in a white environment. . . .
>
> We [the members of the NABSW] have committed ourselves to go back to our communities and work to end this particular form of genocide [transracial adoption].[2]

In his testimony before a Senate committee on June 25, 1985, Merritt reiterated the NABSW position:

> We are opposed to transracial adoption as a solution to permanent placement for Black children. We have an ethnic, moral and professional obligation to oppose transracial adoption. We are therefore *legally* justified in our efforts to protect the right of Black children, Black families, and the Black community. We view the placement of Black children in White homes as a hostile act against our community. It is a blatant form of race and cultural genocide.[3]

In addition, Merritt made the following claims:

- Black children who grow up in white families suffer severe identity problems. On the one hand, the white community has not

fully accepted them; and on the other hand, they have no significant contact with black people.

- Black children adopted transracially often do not develop the
coping mechanisms necessary to function in a society that is inherently racist against African Americans.
- Transracial adoptions, in the long term, often end in disruption;
and the black children are returned to foster care.

Merritt provided no evidence for the claims cited above.

At the annual meeting of the Black Adoption Committee for Kids
on November 8, 1991, another former president of the National Association of Black Social Workers, Morris Jeff, Jr., stated:

> Placing African-American children in white European-American homes
> is an overt hostility, the ultimate insult to black heritage. It is the creation
> of a race of children with African faces and European minds. It is a sim-
> ple answer to a complex situation. It causes more problems than it
> solves.[4]

In 1974, the Black Caucus of the North American Conference on
Adoptable Children recommended "support [for] the consciousness
development movement of all groups" and "that every possible attempt should be made to place black and other minority children in a
cultural and racial setting similar to their original group."[5] In May
1975, the dean of the Howard University School of Social Work and
president of the NABSW stated that "black children who grow up in
white homes end up with white psyches."[6]

In one of the more moderate attacks on transracial adoption, Leon
Chestang in 1972 posed a series of critical questions for white parents
who had adopted or who were considering adopting a black child.

> The central focus of concern in biracial adoption should be the prospec-
> tive adoptive parents. Are they aware of what they are getting into? Do
> they view their act as purely humanitarian, divorced from its social con-
> sequences? Such a response leaves the adoptive parents open to an over-
> whelming shock when friends and family reject and condemn them. Are
> they interested in building world brotherhood without recognizing the
> personal consequences for the child placed in such circumstances? Such

people are likely to be well meaning but unable to relate to the child's individual needs. Are the applicants attempting to solve a personal or social problem through biracial adoption? Such individuals are likely to place an undue burden on the child in resolving their problems.[7]

And what of the implications for the adoptive family itself, of living with a child of another race? Chestang asked. Are negative societal traits attributed to blacks likely to be passed on to the adoptive family, thereby subjecting the family to insults, racial slurs, and ostracism?

> The white family that adopts a black child is no longer a "white family." In the eyes of the community, its members become traitors, nigger-lovers, do-gooders, rebels, oddballs, and, most significantly, ruiners of the community. Unusual psychological armaments are required to shield oneself from the behavioral and emotional onslaught of these epithets.[8]

But Chestang concluded his piece on a more optimistic note than most critics of transracial adoption. "Who knows what problems will confront the black child reared by a white family and what the outcome will be?" he asked. "But these children, if they survive, have the potential for becoming catalysts for society in general."[9]

Most black writers opposed to transracial adoption challenged two main hypotheses: (1) that there are insufficient black adoptive parents willing to adopt black children; and (2) that the benefits a black child will receive in a white family surpass those received in an institution. They observed that many potential nonwhite adoptive parents are disqualified because of adoption agencies' widespread use of white middle-class selection criteria. They also noted that historically, blacks have adopted on an informal basis, preferring not to rely on agencies and courts for sanction. Therefore, the figures cited by agencies cannot reflect the actual number of black adoptions. And they claimed that no longitudinal outcome data were available to show that transracial adoption of black children outweighed the known disadvantages of an institution or foster care; they predicted family and personal problems as the children grew into preadolescence and adolescence. A leading black organization pointed to transracially adopted black children who were returned to foster care because the adoption was not "working out" or who were placed in residential treatment by their white adoptive parents who could not manage them.

Amuzie Chimuzie attributed "all consciously motivating human actions"—for example, transracial adoption—to "selfish needs."[10] He argued that young children are rarely consulted when a major decision is to be made in their lives and that this sense of powerlessness is exacerbated for a young black child in a white adoptive family. Chimuzie suggested,

> It seems appropriate that blacks collectively as parents should speak for the black child in matters touching transracial adoption. . . . It is up to the agent of the child—in this instance blacks as a group—to accept or reject it [transracial adoption]. . . . [I]t has not been determined whether a majority of the blacks are for or against transracial adoption of black children.[11]

One of the most prevalent arguments against transracial adoption is that white families—no matter how liberal or well-meaning—cannot teach a black child how to survive in an essentially racist society. Nonwhites opposed to transracial adoption insist that, because white adoptive parents are not black and cannot experience minority black status, they will rear a psychologically defenseless individual, incapable of understanding and dealing with the racism that exists in our society. Amuzie Chimuzie articulated this position when he emphasized the fear of black social workers and other experts in the child-rearing field that black children reared in white homes will not develop the characteristics needed to survive and flourish in a predominantly white society. After first observing that children tend to acquire most of the psychological and social characteristics of the families and communities in which they are reared, Chimuzie added, "It is therefore possible that black children reared in white families and communities will develop antiblack psychological and social characteristics."[12]

Some black professionals argue that there is a major bottleneck in the placement of black children in black adoptive homes, and this is because child welfare agencies are staffed mainly by white social workers who exercise control over adoptions. The fact that these white agencies are in the position of recruiting and approving black families for adoption causes some blacks to argue that there is institutional racism on the part of the whites. In contrast, there have been several instances where concerted efforts by black child welfare agencies to locate and approve adoptive black families resulted in the adoption of comparatively large numbers of parentless black children.

The previous position was strongly argued by Evelyn Moore, executive director of the National Black Child Development Institute.[13] In an extensive interview about the child welfare system published by the National Association of Social Workers (NASW) in April 1984—a significant part of which dealt either directly or indirectly with transracial adoption—Moore said that 83 percent of all child welfare workers in the United States are white, while 30 to 40 percent of their cases deal with black families. This skewed ratio, she contends, is one of the reasons that there are so few inracial black adoptions. "The adoption system in this country was established to provide white children to white families. As a result, most people who work in the system know very little about black culture or the black community."[14]

Moore also argued that "white middle-class standards" are largely responsible for the rejection of lower-class and working-class black families as potential adopters; they are instead encouraged to become foster parents: "While black children under the age of 19 represent only 14 percent of the children in America, they represent 33 percent of all children not living with their birth parents" (e.g., in foster care or institutionalized).[15]

Two studies conducted by the National Urban League in 1984 are cited by black professionals and organizations as further evidence of the likelihood that institutional racism is one of the primary reasons that more black children are not given to prospective black adoptive families.[16] These studies reported that, of 800 black families applying for adoptive parent status, only two families were approved—0.25 percent—as compared to a national average of 10 percent. Another study concluded that 40 to 50 percent of the black families sampled would consider adoption. An acceptance rate of 0.25 percent becomes somewhat more dramatic when compared to black in-racial adoption rates of 18 per 10,000 families. (The figures for whites and Hispanics are 4 and 3 per 10,000 families, respectively.)

In a 1987 *Ebony* article entitled "Should Whites Adopt Black Children?" the president of the NABSW was quoted as follows: "Our position is that the African-American family should be maintained and its integrity preserved. We see the lateral transfer of black children to white families as contradictory to our preservation efforts."[17]

In 1986, the founder of Homes for Black Children—a successful black adoption agency in Detroit—issued the following statement:

> I believe it was the convergence of these two diverse movements, the transracial adoption movement and the one on the part of Black people to affirm our ability to care for ourselves and our children . . . that resulted in the clash. . . .
>
> For those of us who are Black, the pain has been the fear of losing control of our own destiny through the loss of our children. . . .
>
> . . . [T]here is real fear, in the hearts of some of us who are Black, as to whether a child who is Black can be protected in this society, without the protection of families who are most like him. . . . [A] Black child is especially endangered when agencies or programs that are successful in finding Black families are not available to meet his need.[18]

The winter 1989 newsletter of Homes for Black Children carried a response to the previous statement, written by a member of an Ohio organization called Adopting Older Kids.

> Nowhere in this statement is there acknowledgement of the adoptive parents whose love transcends racial boundaries. . . . Nor are there suggestions about the future of those minority children, already waiting for families, who will be denied loving homes because agencies refuse to consider transracial placements.[19]

How can one explain the discrepancy between the apparently widespread desire to adopt among blacks and the dearth of approved black homes for adoption? First of all, blacks have not adopted in the expected numbers because child welfare agencies have not actively recruited in black communities, using community resources, the black media, and churches. Second, there is a historic suspicion of public agencies among many blacks, the consequence of which is that many restrict their involvement with them. Third, many blacks feel that, no matter how close they come to fulfilling the criteria established for adoption, the fact that they reside in less-affluent areas makes it unlikely that they would be approved.

In 1987, the Council for a Black Economic Agenda—a group dedicated to advancing social welfare policies relevant to the black community—met with President Ronald Reagan to discuss what they and other black groups see as unfair practices on the part of adoption agencies. Urging that eligibility criteria for adoption such as marital status, income, and adoption fees be re-examined with an eye toward more black-oriented standards, they said, "The kind of standards that are being applied by these traditional agencies discriminate against Black parents."[20]

In a 1991 survey conducted by the North American Council on Adoptable Children (NACAC), they reported that 83 percent of the agencies in the twenty-five states studied acknowledged that organizational barriers continued to exist that prevented or discouraged families of color from adopting.[21] The same survey reported that seventeen agencies specializing in finding same-race adoptive placement for children of color found that these agencies located same-race placement for 94 percent of their 341 African-American children and 66 percent of their 38 Hispanic children. Nonspecializing agencies obtained an average of 51 percent of same-race placement—that is, 80 percent of African-American children and 30 percent of Hispanic children.[22]

Hollingsworth also cites research that suggests "that family preservation services may result in fewer placements to families of color compared to white families. Among families in Washington State only 18.2 percent (10 out of 55) families of color who received family preservation services required the out of home placement of children compared with 29.8 percent (75 out of 252) of white families who received these services."[23]

NATIVE-AMERICAN OPPOSITION

The case of Native Americans is a special one. Native Americans have been subjected to a singularly tragic fate, and their children have been particularly vulnerable.

By the early 1970s, committees of Native Americans joined in the denunciation of transracial adoption. In 1972, a group of Native Americans issued the following statement:

> The identity crisis of adolescence is likely to be especially traumatic for the Indian child growing up in a white home. When they are old enough to realize that they're different, there is likely to be real trouble, especially if White parents haven't made serious efforts to expose them to their own cultural heritage. . . . And trouble will come from the White family, too, they say. The White man's hatred of the native American may be forgotten when he's a cute helpless baby or child, but it will show up when the child becomes an adolescent and able to think and act as an individual.[24]

In 1978 Congress passed the Indian Child Welfare Act (P.L. 95-608)—cited in chapter 2—which was designed to prevent the decimation of Indian tribes and the breakdown of Indian families by transracial placement of Native-American children.

In essence, the leaders of black American and Native-American organizations argued that nonwhite children who are adopted by white parents are lost to the communities into which they were born. The experience of growing up in a white world makes it impossible for black and Indian children ever to take their rightful place in the communities of their birth.

CONCLUDING REMARKS

Very few, if any, responsible organizations or individuals argue that transracial adoption is preferable to inracial adoption. Were there sufficient black families for all black children, Hispanic families for Hispanic children, Asian families for Asian children, and so forth, there probably would be no need for transracial adoption. Efforts should be increased to locate minority families—and especially black families—for these children. Those efforts will no doubt be welcomed and supported by all reasonable people. "Traditional" agency policies and practices based on bygone white middle-class assumptions should be altered to meet the current realities of nonwhite communities, thereby increasing the likelihood that larger numbers of potential minority adopters would be located. Such alterations in policies should be promoted by child welfare advocates.

Most—if not all—who see transracial adoption as a viable arrangement see it only when a child's only other options are nonpermanent types of placements such as foster care or group homes. In fact, rarely (if ever) are arguments heard in favor of transracial adoption that do not define it as second-best to permanent inracial placement and do not also include strong support for community agencies to recruit minority adoptive parents vigorously. Witness the following declarations.

The Child Welfare League of America (CWLA), in its most recently published *Standards for Adoption Service,* reaffirmed once again, as it has consistently done in the past, that transracial adoption should be considered only after all efforts at inracial placement have been exhausted. Under the title "Factors in Selection of Family: Ethnicity and Race," the standards read as follows:

> Children in need of adoption have a right to be placed into a family that reflects their ethnicity or race. Children should not have their adoption denied or significantly delayed, however, when adoptive parents of other ethnic or racial groups are available.
>
> . . . In any adoption plan, however, the best interests of the child should be paramount. If aggressive, ongoing recruitment efforts are unsuccessful in finding families of the same ethnicity or culture, other families should be considered.[25]

Another example in which transracial adoption is the second choice to inracial placements appears in a statement made by Father George Clements, a noted black clergyman and founder of "One Church, One Child," a national plan whereby one family from each black church would adopt a black child. After stating that inracial adoptions were preferable to transracial adoption, Father Clements added, "But you cannot always have the ideal, and in lieu of the ideal, I certainly would opt for an Anglo couple, or whatever nationality, taking a child in."[26]

In 1994 the National Association of Black Social Workers issued its current position on transracial adoption. It stated,

> Transracial adoption of an African-American child should only be considered after documented evidence of unsuccessful same-race placement

has been reviewed and supported by appropriate representatives of the African-American community. Under no circumstances should successful same-race placements be impeded by obvious barriers (i.e. legal limits of states, state boundaries, fees, surrogate payment, intrusive applications, lethargic court systems, inadequate staffing patterns, etc.).[27]

The Policy Statement of the National Association of Social Workers issued in 1997 stated its position on transracial adoption as follows:

> Placement decisions should reflect a child's need for continuity safeguarding the child's right to consistent care and to service arrangements. Agencies must recognize each child's need to retain a significant engagement with his or her parents and extended family and respect the integrity of each child's ethnicity and cultural heritage.
>
> The social workers' profession stresses this importance of ethnic and cultural sensitivity. An effort to maintain a child's identity and her or his ethnic heritage should prevail in all services and placement actions that involve children in foster care and adoption programs, including adherence to the principles articulated in the Indian Child Welfare Act.
>
> The recruitment of and placement with adoptive parents from each relevant ethnic or racial group should be available to meet the needs of children.[28]

By the end of the 1990s, it is clear that the major child welfare and social work organizations still remain strongly committed to the idea of recruiting minority adoptive parents for minority children. They all emphasize the importance of ethnic heritage and that efforts should be made to ensure that adoptive parents of the same race as the child are available. In all likelihood, these groups would abandon support for transracial adopting wherever there is a sufficient number of racially similar parents to accommodate waiting nonwhite children.

NOTES

1. William T. Merritt, speech to the National Association of Black Social Workers National Conference, Washington, D.C., 1971.

2. Ibid.

3. Excerpt from testimony by William T. Merritt, president of the National Association of Black Social Workers, Senate Hearings, Committee on Labor and Human Resources, June 25, 1985.

4. Morris Jeff, Jr., "Interracial Adoptions Wrong, Says Official," *St. Louis Post Dispatch,* November 9, 1991.

5. "Barriers to Same Race Placement," report of the North American Council on Adoptable Children (St. Paul, Minn., 1991).

6. Sandy Barnesky, "The Question: Is It Bad for Black Children to Be Adopted by Whites?," *Baltimore Sun,* May 28, 1975, p. B1.

7. Leon Chestang, "The Dilemma of Bi-Racial Adoption," *Social Work* (May 1972): 100–105.

8. Ibid., p. 103.

9. Ibid., p. 105.

10. Amuzie Chimuzie, "Transracial Adoption of Black Children," *Social Work* (July 1975): 296–301.

11. Ibid., p. 298.

12. Ibid., p. 300.

13. Evelyn Moore, "Black Children Facing Adoption Barriers," *NASW News* (April 1984): 9.

14. Ibid., p. 9.

15. Ibid., p. 10.

16. Ibid., p. 11.

17. Morris Jeff, "Should Whites Adopt Black Children?," *Ebony* (September 1987): 78.

18. Statement in *Homes for Black Children,* newsletter of Homes for Black Children (Detroit, Mich., 1986).

19. *Homes for Black Children* (Winter 1989).

20. Council for a Black Economic Agenda, press release on meeting with President Ronald Reagan (Washington, D.C., 1987).

21. Leslie Doty Hollingsworth, "Promoting Same-Race Adoption for Children of Color," *Social Work,* vol. 43, no. 2 (March 1998): 108.

22. Ibid., p. 108.

23. Ibid., p. 110.

24. *Ann Arbor* (Mich.) *News,* July 1972, p. 10.

25. *Standards for Adoption Service* (New York: Child Welfare League of America, 1988).

26. Statement of Father George Clements, *The National Adoption Report,* vol. 10, no. 3., Washington, D.C. (May–June 1989).

27. National Association of Black Social Workers Position Statement (Detroit, 1994).

28. National Association of Social Workers, "Social Work Speaks" (Washington, D.C.: NASW Press, 1977).

4

✛

Results of Empirical Studies of Transracial Adoptions

The work of Lucille Grow and Deborah Shapiro of the Child Welfare League represents one of the earliest studies of transracial adoption. Published in 1974, the main purpose of *Black Children, White Parents* was to assess how successful the adoption of black children by white parents had been.[1] Their respondents consisted of 125 families.

On the basis of the children's scores on the California Test of Personality (which purports to measure social and personal adjustment), Grow and Shapiro concluded that the children in their study made about as successful an adjustment in their adoptive homes as other nonwhite children had in prior studies. They claimed that 77 percent of their children had adjusted successfully and that this percentage was similar to that reported in other studies. Grow and Shapiro also compared the scores of transracially adopted children with those of adopted white children on the California Test of Personality. A score below the twentieth percentile was defined as reflecting poor adjustment, and a score above the fiftieth percentile was defined as indicating good adjustment. They found that the scores of their transracially adopted children and those of white adopted children matched very closely.

In 1977, Joyce Ladner—using the membership lists of the Open

Door Society and the Council on Adoptable Children as her sample frames—conducted in-depth interviews with 136 parents in Georgia; Missouri; Washington, D.C.; Maryland; Virginia; Connecticut; and Minnesota.[2] Before reporting her findings, she introduced a personal note:

> This research brought with it many self-discoveries. My initial feelings were mixed. I felt some trepidation about studying white people, a new undertaking for me. Intellectual curiosity notwithstanding, I had the gnawing sensation that I shouldn't delve too deeply because the findings might be too controversial. I wondered too if couples I intended to interview would tell me the truth. Would some lie in order to cover up their mistakes and disappointments with the adoption? How much would they leave unsaid? Would some refuse to be interviewed because of their preconceived notions about my motives? Would they stereotype me as a hostile black sociologist who wanted to "prove" that these adoptions would produce unhealthy children?[3]

By the end of the study, Ladner was convinced that "there are whites who are capable of rearing emotionally healthy black children." Such parents, Ladner continued, "must be idealistic about the future but also realistic about the society in which they now live."

> To deny racial, ethnic, and social class polarization exists, and to deny that their child is going to be considered a "black child," regardless of how light his or her complexion, how sharp their features, or how straight their hair, means that these parents are unable to deal with reality, as negative as they may perceive that reality to be. On the other hand, it is equally important for parents to recognize that no matter how immersed they become in the black experience, they can never become black. Keeping this in mind, they should avoid the pitfalls of trying to practice an all-black lifestyle, for it too is unrealistic in the long run, since their family includes blacks and whites and should, therefore, be part of the larger black and white society.[4]

Charles Zastrow's doctoral dissertation, published in 1977, compared the reactions of forty-one white couples who had adopted a black child against a matched sample of forty-one white couples who had adopted a white child.[5] All of the families lived in Wisconsin. The two groups were matched on the age of the adopted child and on the socioeconomic status of the adoptive parent. All of the children in the study were preschoolers. The overall findings indicated that the outcomes of the transracial (TRA) placements were as successful as the inracial (IRA) placements. And Zastrow commented:

> One of the most notable findings is that TRA parents reported considerably fewer problems related to the care of the child have arisen than they anticipated prior to the adoption. . . . Many of the TRA couples mentioned that they became "color-blind" shortly after adopting; i.e., they stopped seeing the child as a black, and came to perceive the child as an individual who is a member of their family.[6]

When the parents were asked to rate their overall satisfaction with the adoptive experience, 99 percent of the TRA parents and 100 percent of the IRA parents checked "extremely satisfying" or "more satisfying than dissatisfying." And on another measure of satisfaction—one in which the parents rated their degree of satisfaction with certain aspects of their adoptive experience—out of a possible maximum of 98 points, the mean score of the TRA parents was 92.1 and the IRA parents, 92.0.

Using a mail survey in 1981, William Feigelman and Arnold Silverman compared the adjustment of fifty-six black children adopted by white families against ninety-seven white children adopted by white families.[7] The parents were asked to assess their child's overall adjustment and to indicate the frequency with which their child demonstrated emotional and physical problems. Silverman and Feigelman concluded that the child's age—not the transracial adoption—had the most significant impact on development and adjustment. The older the child, the greater the problems. They found no relationship between adjustment and racial identity.

W. M. Womak and W. Fulton's study of transracial adoptees and nonadopted black preschool children found no significant differences in racial attitudes between the two groups of children.[8]

In 1983, Ruth McRoy and Louis Zurcher reported the findings of their study of thirty black adolescents who had been transracially adopted and thirty black adolescents who had been adopted by black parents.[9]

In the concluding chapter of their book, McRoy and Zurcher wrote:

> The transracial and inracial adoptees in the authors' study were physically healthy and exhibited typical adolescent relationships with their parents, siblings, teachers, and peers. Similarly, regardless of the race of their adoptive parents, they reflected positive feelings of self-regard.[10]

Throughout the book, the authors emphasized that the quality of parenting was more important than whether the black child had been inracially or transracially adopted: "Most certainly, transracial adoptive parents experience some challenges different from inracial adoptive parents, but in this study, all of the parents successfully met the challenges."[11]

In 1988, Joan Shireman and Penny Johnson described the results of their study involving twenty-six inracial (black) and twenty-six transracial adoptive families in Chicago.[12] They reported very few differences between the two groups of eight-year-old adoptees. Using the Clark and Clark Doll Test to establish racial identity, 73 percent of the transracial adopted identified themselves as black, compared to 80 percent for the inracially adopted black children. The authors concluded that 75 percent of the transracial adoptees and 80 percent of the inracial adoptees appeared to be doing quite well. They also commented that the transracial adoptees had developed pride in being black and were comfortable in their interactions with both black and white races.

In a 1992 unpublished report, Karen Vroegh—a researcher in the Shireman and Associates project—concluded:

> The majority of the adopted adolescents, whether TRA or IRA (inracially adopted) were doing well. The rate and type of identified problems were similar to those found in the general population. Over 90 percent of the TRA parents thought transracial adoption was a good idea.[13]

In 1988, Richard Barth reported that transracial placements were no more likely to be disruptive than other types of adoptions.[14] The fact that transracial placements were as stable as other, more traditional, adoptive arrangements was reinforced by data presented in 1988 at a North American Council on Adoptable Children (NACAC) meeting on adoption disruption. There it was reported that the rate of adoption disruptions averaged about 15 percent. Disruptions, they reported, did not appear to be influenced by the adoptees' race or gender or the fact that they were placed as a sibling group.

In 1993, Christopher Bagley compared a group of twenty-seven transracial adoptees with a group of twenty-five inracially adopted whites. Both sets of adoptees were approximately nineteen years old and were on average about two years old when adopted.[15] Bagley concluded his study with the following statement:

> The findings of the present study underscore those from previous American research on transracial adoption. Transracial adoption . . . appears to meet the psychosocial and developmental needs of the large majority of the children involved, and can be just as successful as inracial adoption.[16]

In January 1999, Devon Brooks and Richard Barth reported some of the findings of their ongoing longitudinal study begun in 1977 of 144 Asian, 41 white, and 39 African-American adoptees. The authors reported that being the only adopted child in a family of birth children, and being a male adoptee, especially a white male, were negatively related to adjustment. Racial differences between the adoptees and their parents did not factor into overall adjustment patterns. The adoptees' average age was mid-twenties.[17]

NATIVE-AMERICAN TRANSRACIAL ADOPTIONS

Even though the research by David Fanshel reported in *Far from the Reservation* was conducted almost thirty years ago, it still remains the definitive study of the experiences of transracially adopted Native-American children and is therefore worth noting.[18]

On the whole, Fanshel saw in the results of his study grounds for cautious optimism. In table 4.1, we see that he divided his families

Table 4.1   Level of Adjustment Perceived by White Parents of American-Indian Children, Fanshel Study

N	Percent	Description of Level
10	10	*Level One* (Child is making an excellent adjustment in all spheres—the outlook for his future adjustment is *excellent*.)
41	43	*Level Two*
24	25	*Level Three* (Child is making an adequate adjustment—his strengths outweigh the weaknesses he shows—the outlook for his future adjustment is *hopeful*.)
10	10	*Level Four*
10	10	*Level Five* (Child is making a mixed adjustment—generally the problems he faces are serious and the outlook for his future adjustment is *guarded*.)
1	1	*Level Six*
None	None	*Level Seven* (Child is making an extremely poor adjustment—the outlook for his future adjustment is *unpromising*.)

Source: David Fanshel, *Far from the Reservation: The Transracial Adoption of American Indian Children* (Metuchen, N.J.: Scarecrow Press, 1972), p. 280.

into seven adjustment levels and distributed them according to the degree to which the parents reported that they believed their adopted child had made the adjustment described at each level.

The distribution shows that only 10 percent of the parents perceived their children's future adjustment as "guarded" (Level 5), and only one child was seen to have a "dim" (Level 6) future. In Fanshel's words:

> More than fifty percent of the children were rated as showing relatively problem-free adjustments (Levels 1 and 2) and another twenty-five percent were rated as showing adequate adjustment with strengths outweighing weaknesses (Level 3). Another ten percent of the children were rated at Level 4—located midway between adjustment regarded as adequate and those viewed as guarded.[19]

Many of the parents acknowledged that difficulties lay ahead and that they expected those difficulties to surface when their children reached adolescence and adulthood. Many felt that the difficulties should be proportional to the "full-bloodedness" of their children, and the children who appeared less distinctively Indian would have less-turbulent experiences. The existence of anxiety or lack of it therefore rested on the degree to which the children were of mixed blood.

In examining which social and demographic factors correlated best with the parents' perceptions of the child's adjustment, Fanshel found the strongest relationship between age and adjustment. The older the child at the time of initial placement, the more difficult the adjustment. Fanshel also discovered an association between age at placement and parental strictness, noting that the older the child, the more strict the adoptive parents tended to be.

It is important to emphasize that all these impressions were based on the *parents'* responses to their children's adjustment over three different time periods. A professional evaluation of parental impressions (referred to as the "overall child adjustment rating") was the yardstick by which the children's adjustment was viewed, and it served as the basis of predictions for the future. At no time did Fanshel involve the children in attempting to predict future adjustment.

In his conclusion, Fanshel addressed the issue of whether the transracial adoption of American-Indian children should be encouraged. He described the costs involved in transracial adoption and concluded that adoption was cheaper than foster care or institutionalization. He established that the children were secure and loved in their adoptive homes. He found that the adoptive parents were happy and satisfied with their children. Nevertheless, in the end, he concluded that the decision as to whether the practice should or should not continue would be made on political grounds and not on the basis of the quality of the adjustment that parents and children experienced.

THE SIMON-ALTSTEIN TWENTY-YEAR STUDY[20]

In 1971–1972, Rita Simon contacted 206 families living in five cities in the Midwest who were members of the Open Door Society and the Council on Adoptable Children (COAC) and asked whether she could interview them about their decision to adopt a nonwhite child. All of the families but two (who declined for reasons unrelated to adoption) agreed to participate in the study. The parents allowed a two-person team composed of one male and one female graduate student to interview them in their home for 60–90 minutes at the same time that each of their children, who were between four and seven years old, was being interviewed for about 30 minutes. In total, 204 parents and 366 children were interviewed. The distribution by race, sex, and adoptive status is described in table 4.2.

Seven years later, we (Rita Simon and Howard Altstein) sought out these families again and were able to locate 71 percent of them. The remaining 29 percent of the families were unreachable through any of the channels we tried. We contacted local chapters of the Open Door Society and COAC officers and consulted membership lists of various other transracial adoption organizations. We asked for information from people who had helped us seven years earlier. All of our leads resulted in returned "undeliverable" envelopes. While it is unfortunate that we were unable to locate all of the original families, we were gratified that we could reach 71 percent of them seven years later. Of the families we did reach, 93 percent agreed to participate in the second survey. Ten of the 143 families did not. The interviews at that time—which were done only with the parents and by mail or phone—focused on their relationships with their adopted child(ren) and with the children born to them, on the children's racial identity, and on the ties that both the adopted and the nonadopted children had to their larger family units (i.e., grandparents, aunts, and uncles), their schools, and their communities.

In the fall of 1983 and the winter of 1984, the families were contacted

Table 4.2   Racial, Sexual, and Adoptive Status of Children Subjects

	Adopted		Born to Family		
Racial Background	*Boys*	*Girls*	*Boys*	*Girls*	*Total*
White	21	21	100	67	209
Black	75	45	—	—	120
American Indian, Asian, etc.	16	21	—	—	37
Total	112	87	100	67	366

a third time. We returned to our original design and conducted personal interviews in the respondents' homes, with both the parents and the adolescent adopted and birth children.

Of the 133 families who participated in the 1979 study, 88 took part in the 1984 survey. In addition, 8 families who had participated in the 1971 study, but could not be found in 1979, were located in 1984 and participated. From among the 133 families who had been involved in the 1979 study, 28 moved and could not be located; or in a few cases, when we did find them, we could not arrange to interview them. In one family, the only child who was transracially adopted had died in an auto accident. Eleven families declined to be interviewed; and in one city, the interviewing team did not complete the scheduled interviews, and we thereby lost five families.

The refusal rate of 10 percent—while still low—was slightly higher than the 7 percent we had in 1979. Among the eleven families who did not wish to be interviewed, two had been divorced since 1979. The family members were separated, and some of them did not wish to "get involved." Three families had been interviewed by other researchers and felt that "enough is enough." The members of one family said that they had gone through a number of family problems recently and that this was not a good time for them. The other five families gave no reason.

Going back to the 1979 profiles of the eleven families who declined to be interviewed in 1983–1984, we found that in five of the families the parents described problems between themselves and their children. These problems included the following: The child had a "learning disability that put a lot of stress on the family"; the child was "hyperactive and was experiencing identity problems"; the child was "retarded and was having personality problems"; the child had "a severe learning disability and behavioral problems that [affected] school performance"; and "the adoption has not been accepted by the extended family." Another set of parents, who characterized their relations with their transracially adopted child as "negative," traced the problems to a brain injury that had resulted from an automobile accident.

In five families, the parents agreed to be interviewed but—for a variety of reasons—did not allow their children to participate. Among the reasons given were the following: Only the transracially adopted children were still at home, and the parents felt that they were too young (fourteen and fifteen years old) to go through an interview that probed into the areas we were covering; the children did not seem interested, and the parents did not want to pressure them; and, in one family, the only child still at home stated specifically that she did not want to be interviewed.

In total, the 96 families had 394 children, consisting of 213 boys and 181 girls; 256 were still living at home, and 34 were away at school but considered the parents' home their home. The others had moved away, were working, or were married. Forty-three percent of all the children had been transracially adopted.

We interviewed 218 children. They represented 55 percent of the total number of children born to or adopted by the parents and 85 percent of the children still living at home. Of the 34 children who were attending colleges or universities and considered their parents' home their official residence, we were able to interview a few when they were home on vacation. Some of the children remaining at home were too young (not yet adolescents) to be included in this phase of the study. Fifty-four percent of those at home were transracially adopted. Among the transracial adoptees, we interviewed 61 boys and 50 girls, or 80 percent of those at home. Eighty-nine of the 111 TRAs were American black. The others were Korean, Native American, Eskimo, or Vietnamese. We also interviewed 48 males and 43 females who were born into the families and 4 males and 12 females who are white adoptees.

The third survey focused on how the family members related to each other, the racial identities of the adopted children, the adopted children's sense of integration with their families, and the parents' and children's expectations concerning the children's future identity. We asked about the bonds that the TRAs were likely to have toward the mainly white-oriented world of their parents and siblings and the ties that the TRAs were likely to develop with the community of their racial and ethnic backgrounds or with some composite world.

The fourth phase of the study began in 1991. We were able to locate eighty-three of the ninety-six families who had participated in the 1984 study. Of those eighty-three families, seventy-six (92 percent) provided us with the names and addresses of their adult transracially adopted and birth children. Seven families opted not to participate. In 1993, we reviewed the interviews we had conducted with those seven families and found nothing unusual in them. One set of parents had divorced in 1974; the two children—one adopted and one birth child—were living with the mother; the father saw them on weekends and holidays. The relationships between the parents and children in the other six families were all intact. The children were attending universities or high schools. There was no mention by the parents or the children of physical or emotional/mental illnesses or of drug or alcohol use. Those families who offered an explanation for their unwillingness to participate said their children "weren't particularly interested" or that "they had a busy schedule and did not want to take the time." Of the remaining seventy-six families, four had children who were still in high school, and we chose not to interview them.

MAJOR FINDINGS

Family Characteristics

When we examined the parents' responses to the initial interview schedule in 1972, we were struck by the homogeneity of the families' social and economic status. Their educational backgrounds, for example, showed that at least 62 percent of the mothers had completed four years of college and 28 percent of them had continued on to graduate school. Sixty-one percent of the fathers worked as professionals. Most of them were ministers, social workers, or academicians. Among the remaining third, 12 percent were businessmen, and the other 20 percent were clerical workers, salesmen, skilled laborers, or graduate students.

None of the mothers held full-time jobs outside their homes. Almost all of them explained that when they and their husbands made the decision to adopt, this also involved a commitment on the wife's part to remain at home in the role of full-time mother. Before they were married, or before they adopted their first child, 46 percent of the mothers had held jobs in a professional capacity, and 3 percent had been enrolled as graduate students. About 14 percent did not work outside the home before they gave birth to, or adopted, their first child. The parents' median income in 1972 was $16,500.

By current standards the fact that so many mothers in our study chose to remain at home may seem somewhat incongruous, given that almost half of them held full-time jobs outside their homes before marriage or adoption. But it should be remembered that our initial interviews with these families took place in the early 1970s, a time not only when many more women saw their role as full-time mother but also when criteria for adoption approval rested to a large degree on the extent to which the mother (not father or parent) remained at home in the capacity of full-time, in-home caretaker.

The average age of the mother was 34 and that of the father, 36. The range for both parents in 1972 was between 25 and 50. They had been married for an average of 12 years; the shortest time was 2 years and the longest was 25 years.

The Midwest is heavily Protestant, and so were the respondents in our sample. Sixty-three percent of the mothers and 57 percent of the fathers acknowledged belonging to some Protestant congregation. Lutheranism was cited by 19 percent of both mothers and fathers. Twenty-one percent of the mothers and 22 percent of the fathers were Catholics, 1 and 2 percent were Jewish, and the remaining 15 and 19 percent acknowledged no formal religious identification or affiliation. Most of the parents who acknowledged a religious affiliation also said they attended church regularly, at least once a week. The church played an important role in the lives of many of these families. Some parents reported that much of their social life was organized around their church and that many of their friends belonged to it—especially other families who had adopted nonwhite children.

Political affiliations and activities were not as important as the church for most of the families. About a third of the parents described themselves as independents, about 40 percent as Democrats, and 12 percent as Republicans; the others had no preference or named a local party (in Minnesota, the Farmer Labor party) as the one they generally supported or had voted for in the previous election. Only a small proportion—less than a quarter of the group—said that they belonged to a local political club or that they worked for a political candidate.

The number of children per family ranged from one to seven; this included birth as well as adopted children. Nineteen percent of the parents did not have any birth children. All of those families reported that they were unable to bear children.

The families who adopted more than three children were in almost all instances those in which the father or both parents were professionally involved in adoption services, youth work, or social work. They had prior experience as foster parents, and some had foster children currently living with them. In a sense, their decision to adopt and their plans to make themselves available as foster parents were part of their professional roles.

Twenty-six percent of the families adopted their first child. Since 19 percent of these parents were unable to bear children, it turns out that only 7 percent of those who had children born to them had adopted their first child. In many cases, the fact that parents who were not infertile had children born to them before they adopted was not a matter of choice but a reflection of the policy of the adoption agency with which they were dealing. Unless couples could produce medical evidence that they were unable to bear a child, most of them were "strongly advised" to have at least one child; and then, if they were still interested in adoption, the agency would be willing to consider their candidacy.

Twenty-six percent of the time, the first adopted child was the oldest child in the family; 32 percent of the time, she or he was the middle child; and 41 percent of the time, he or she was the youngest child. Among those families who adopted more than one child (56 percent), the second adopted child occupied the "middle" position 35 percent of the time and the "youngest" position 65 percent of the time. American blacks made up the largest category of adopted children. They also comprised the category of children who were the most available for adoption.

Among those families who adopted one child, 56 percent adopted a boy and 44 percent, a girl. Among those families who adopted more than one child, 60 percent adopted boys and girls, 22 percent adopted only boys, and 18 percent adopted only girls. The sex ratio for all the adopted children shows that 41 percent of the families adopted only a boy, 32 percent adopted only a girl, and 27 percent adopted both sexes. The overall pattern thus reveals a slight preference for boys over girls. In almost every instance, when parents expressed a preference for a boy or a girl, it was because they wanted a child to match or complement a desired family pattern. For some, a girl was needed as a sister or a boy was wanted as a brother; for others, there were only boys in the family, and the parents wanted a daughter, or vice versa. In only a few instances did childless parents indicate that they had a sex preference.

Sixty-nine percent of the first-child adoptions were of children less than one year of age, compared to 80 percent of the second-child adoptions. One explanation for the greater proportion of younger adoptions the second time around is that adoption agencies were more likely to provide such families—who had already proven themselves by their successful first adoption—with the most desirable and sought-after children, than they were to place such children in untried homes.

In 1972, only a minority of the families had initially considered adopting a nonwhite child. Most of them said they had wanted a healthy baby. When they found that they could not have a healthy white baby, they sought to adopt a healthy black, Indian, or Korean baby—rather than an older white child or a physically or mentally handicapped white child or baby. They preferred a child of another race to a child whose physical or mental handicaps might cause considerable financial drain or emotional strain. About 40 percent of the families intended or wanted to adopt nonwhite children because of their own involvement in the civil rights movement and as a reflection of their general sociopolitical views.

Of the families that we contacted seven years later, at least a third of the mothers were working full-time outside their homes. For some of them, it was a matter of necessity; for others, it was a matter of choice. Among the women who returned to work by choice, almost all were engaged in professional positions of the type they had left before they adopted their first child. The women who worked out of necessity were divorced and had become the heads of their households. Most held white-collar or secretarial jobs. The majority of the women in the survey chose to remain at home as full-time housewives and mothers.

In 1972, all the families were intact: There were no separations, divorces, or deaths. By 1979, two of the fathers had died. In one family, both parents died, and the older siblings were raising the younger ones. In one family, the parents were separated; and in nineteen families, the parents were divorced. In three of those nineteen, the father had custody of the children.

Twenty-three families adopted one more child after 1972, and twelve families had another child born to them. Of the children adopted after 1972, five were white, eleven were American black, and the other seven were Vietnamese refugees. Thirteen were boys and ten were girls. Eighteen percent of the parents reported that at least one child had left home to attend college or to marry.

In 1972, 78 percent of the survey families were living in all-white neighborhoods. Four percent lived in predominantly black neighborhoods, and the other 18 percent lived in mixed neighborhoods. Among the large majority who lived in all-white neighborhoods, only a few said they planned to move when their adopted children approached school age. Most of the parents saw no incongruity between their family composition and their choice of neighborhood.

Little changed in that respect over the years. In 1979, 77 percent of the families were still living in all-white or predominantly white neighborhoods. The others lived in mixed communities. Several families who lived in white neighborhoods transferred their church memberships to mixed congregations in other neighborhoods. One mother said, "We did this chiefly to give our adopted daughter greater personal acceptance and support there also."

A few of the families who lived in mixed neighborhoods moved there because they wanted a better racial mix for their children. One parent in a mixed neighborhood reported that, of the eight families on their block, four had adopted transracially. Several parents said that they planned to move into a mixed community before their adopted children became teenagers.

On the other hand, one parent said that his family had decided to leave a mixed neighborhood because their children were making such observations as "All blacks steal," and "Most black kids get into trouble with the police." The mixed neighborhood was less affluent than the one in which they had lived previously.

Seventy-one percent of the parents reported that their children attended mixed schools, and 6 percent said the schools were mostly black. With one exception, all the children in this latter category lived with their mothers after their parents had divorced. A lower standard of living, as opposed to a different ideological position or commitment, seemed to be the major factor for the child's attending a predominantly black school.

Eighty-eight percent of both the fathers and mothers participated in the 1983–1984 study. Among the remaining 12 percent, the mother served as the respondent most of the time. Returning to the families four-and-a-half years after our second study, we found that 83 percent of the parents were still married to their original partners; six had divorced before 1979, and two after 1979. Three pairs of parents were separated. Half of the divorced couples had remarried. The mother had custody of the children in four families; the father, in two. There was joint custody in two, and each parent had custody of at least one child in three families. In four of the families, the father died; and in one family, both parents died before 1979 and the children were being reared by older siblings.

In 1984, 72 percent of the mothers were employed full-time outside their homes, almost all of them in technical and white-collar positions as teachers, nurses, and secretaries. Sixty-six percent of the fathers continued to work as professionals, such as lawyers, ministers, teachers, professors, and doctors. Most of the others were in business. The median family income was $44,000.

Ninety-three percent of the families lived in single-dwelling homes in residential neighborhoods. Seventy-three percent of the parents described their neighborhoods as completely or almost completely white. Eighty percent of the parents reported that they had lived in the same house for at least ten years.

In 1983–1984, the TRAs were most likely to be the youngest children still at home—81 percent of them, compared to 17 percent of the children born into the family and 1 percent of the white adoptees. All but four of the TRAs were still in school at the time of the study; fifteen of the children born to the families and four of the white adoptees were no longer in school. Among the children at the precollege level, 83 percent of the TRAs, 82 percent of those born into the family, and 80 percent of the white adoptees were attending public institutions. At the college level as well, most of the children, adoptees and birth, were attending public universities. The racial composition of the schools that the children attended was described by them in table 4.3.

The birth children and the white adoptees were no more likely to have attended the predominantly white schools than were the transracially adopted children.

In 1990–1991, 24 percent of the TRAs and 63 percent of the birth children had thus far completed at least a baccalaureate degree. All but 10 percent of the TRAs said that they planned to go on with their schooling for at least a baccalaureate degree or higher. Among those currently attending colleges or universities, about 60 percent of their parents were paying for tuition, room, and board—for both the TRAs and the birth children.

Forty percent of the birth children and 13 percent of the TRAs were currently married. Of the twelve married birth children, two of their spouses were Asian; among the TRAs, one out of five of the black adopted children was married to a black person, and the other four had white spouses.

Of the TRAs who were currently employed (84 percent), 18 percent were professionals; 20 percent worked in administrative or clerical jobs, and 43 percent in skilled and service jobs; the others were in the armed services or doing other things. All but 3 percent of the birth children were employed—one-third in professional work, one-third in administrative or clerical positions, 17 percent in skilled and service jobs, and 13 percent in other positions.

Sixty percent of the TRAs and 77 percent of the birth children lived in neighborhoods that were mostly white. Fifty-eight percent of the TRAs and 57 percent of the birth children attended the same church as their parents.

Table 4.3   Racial Composition of Schools

	Percent
76–100 percent white	58
51–75 percent white	22
50 percent white	10
Less than 50 percent white	10

THE ADOPTION EXPERIENCE

The most important finding that emerged from our first encounter with the families in 1971–1972 was the absence of a white racial preference or bias on the part of the white birth children and the nonwhite adopted children. When we gave the birth and the adopted children the now-famous Kenneth Clark "doll" test, we found that unlike all other previous doll studies, our respondents did not favor the white doll. It was not considered smarter, prettier, nicer, and so forth, than the black doll by either the white or black children. Neither did the other projective tests conducted during the interview reveal preferences for white or negative reactions to black. Yet the black and white children in our study accurately identified themselves as white or black on those same tests. In writing about these results, we said that transracial adoption appeared to provide the opportunity for children to develop an awareness of race and a respect for physical characteristics, whatever they may be.

When we returned to these families in 1979, we learned that the "extremely glowing, happy portrait" that we had painted seven years earlier now had some blemishes on it. There were signs of stress and tension. We noted that for every five families in which there were the usual pleasures and joys along with sibling rivalries, school-related problems, and difficulties in communication between parent and child, there was one family whose difficulties were more profound and were believed by the parents to be related to the transracial adoption.[21]

The serious problem most frequently cited by the parents was the adopted child's (usually a boy's) tendency to steal from other members of the family. The boys stole money from their mothers' purses and bicycles, clothing, stereos, and money from their siblings. Most often, they simply gave the items away. Was this conduct a function of the children's adopted status, their racial differences, or a combination of both? How long was it likely to continue? Would the children be likely to engage in other forms of delinquent behavior as they grew older? We could find no references to these behaviors in studies that had been done of adopted children, but when we sought out clinicians whose caseloads often involved adoptees, we were told that intrafamily stealing was not unusual. It was the adopted children's form of testing. How much of a commitment did the family have toward them? Were parents prepared to keep them when things got rough, when they did not behave like model children? Were they really part of the family, for better or for worse? Four years later, when we went back to the families for the third time, none of them reported that the stealing had continued. It just stopped.

Our third survey encounter occurred in 1983–1984 when most of the children were adolescents. We found that almost all of the families had made some changes in their lives. Most of the time, however, the changes were not made because they had decided to adopt a child of a different race but because the adoption added another child to the family. Thus, the parents talked about buying a bigger house, adding more bedroom space, having less money for vacations and entertainment, and allowing less time for themselves. In retrospect, most of the parents did not dwell on what they wished they had done but did not do; nor did they berate themselves for things they did and wished they had not done. Most of them felt that they were doing their best. They worked hard at being parents and at being parents to children of a different race.

Many of them were enthusiastic about introducing the culture of the TRA's background into the family's day-to-day life. The parents of black children introduced books about black history and black heroes, joined a black church, sought out black playmates for their children, and celebrated Martin Luther King's birthday. In a few families, black friends became the godparents to their transracially adopted child. One mother told us: "Black parents regard us as black parents." Parents of Korean and Native-American children experimented with new recipes; sought out books, music, and artifacts; joined churches and social organizations; traveled to the Southwest for ethnic ceremonies; and participated in local ethnic events. But as the years progressed, it was the children rather than the parents who were more likely to want to call a halt to these types of activities. "Not every dinner conversation has to be a lesson in black history," or "we are more interested in basketball and football than in ceremonial dances" were the comments we heard frequently from the TRAs as they were growing up.

In the 1983–1984 phase, all of the children were asked to complete a "self-esteem scale," which in essence measures how much respect a respondent has for herself or himself. A person is characterized as having high self-esteem if she or he considers herself or himself to be a person of worth. Low self-esteem means that the individual lacks self-respect. Because we wanted to make the best possible comparison among our respondents, we examined the scores of our black TRAs separately from those of the other TRAs and from those of the white born and white adopted children. As shown in table 4.4, the scores for all four groups were virtually the same. No one group of respondents manifested higher or lower self-esteem than the others.

The Shireman and Associates study also included the self-esteem scale, and they reported that "the majority of the teenage adoptees . . . whether TRA or IRA, black or mixed, have good self-esteem."

The lack of differences among our adolescent responses was again dramatically exemplified in our findings on the "family integration scale," which included such items as the following: "People in our family trust one another"; "My parents know what I am really like as a person"; and "I enjoy family life." The hypothesis was that adopted children would feel less integrated than children born into the families. The scores reported by our four groups of respondents (black TRAs, other TRAs, white born, and white adopted) showed no significant differences; and indeed, among the three largest categories (not including white adoptees), the mean scores measuring family integration were practically identical: 15.4, 15.2, and 15.4.

We believe that one of the important measures of the parents' unselfish love and concern about their adopted children may be found in their responses to the question about the birth parents. Approximately 40 percent of the parents told us that their children expressed

Table 4.4   Self-Esteem Scores

Categories of Respondents	N	Median	Mean	Standard Deviation
Black TRAs	86	17.8	18.1	3.49
Other TRAs	17	18.0	18.3	3.66
White Born	83	18.1	18.0	3.91
White Adopted	15	18.0	18.5	3.16

interest in learning about their birth parents. Of those, 7 percent also wanted to locate and meet one or both of their birth parents. An additional 10 percent of the parents had already provided their adopted children with whatever information they had—even prior to, or in the absence of, the children's request. Out of the 40 percent whose children asked about their birth parents, only three parents were sufficiently threatened by the child's interest to refuse to provide the information they had.

Looking at the issue from the adoptees' perspective, we found that 38 percent of the TRAs had already tried or were planning to try to locate their birth parents. The others said that they had not decided or did not plan to try to find them. The most typical response was: "I am happy with my family. My other parents gave me up." Most of the adoptees did not have deeply rooted feelings about their reasons for wanting to locate their birth parents; curiosity seemed to characterize most of their feelings. Many said, "I would like to see what I will look like when I'm older." Those for whom the issue was more traumatic were children who were adopted when they were three or more years of age, had some memory of a mother, and felt a sense of abandonment or betrayal. They expressed their feelings in this rather muted phrase: "I'll feel incomplete until I do."

In the 1990–1991 study, we began the parents' interview by asking: "Thinking back, and with the knowledge of hindsight and the experiences you have accumulated, would you have done what you did—adopt a child of a different race?" Ninety-two percent of the parents answered yes; 4 percent said they were not sure; and 4 percent said no. Of the families who said no (i.e., they would not have adopted a nonwhite child), two of the three explained that the child they adopted had preexisting physical and emotional problems they were not aware of at the time of adoption and that these problems had made their lives very difficult. Race was not an issue. The other family simply said that in general it was not a successful experience.

We then asked, "With all of the thought and preparation that had gone into your decision to adopt, what was it about the experience that surprised you the most?" The two most frequently offered answers—made by 22 and 21 percent of the parents, respectively—were that "there have been no major surprises" and that "the surprise was how easy or how successful the experience had been." The other two most frequent reactions—each offered by 16 percent of the respondents—were how little information they had been given about their child's physical, emotional, and social backgrounds; and how complicated the teen years were—particularly how their child grappled with identity issues.

Finally, we asked the parents—just as we had asked them twenty and eight years earlier—"Would you recommend that other families like your own adopt a child of a different race?" Eighty percent answered yes; 3 percent said no; and 17 percent were not sure. Twenty years earlier, 90 percent said they would recommend TRA to other families; and eight years earlier, 85 percent said they would.

We were less successful in contacting the children than we were the parents. In 1983, we interviewed 218 children (111 TRAs, 91 birth, and 16 white adoptees). In 1991, we were able to contact and interview 98 children—of whom 55 had been transracially adopted, 30 were birth children, and 13 were white adoptees. We did not try to contact all of the birth children because we thought it more important to interview as many of the adopted—especially the transracially adopted—children as we could locate. While most of the parents stayed put, the children seemed to have been particularly mobile during the period between 1983 and 1991. In large measure, of course, this was a function of their age and status. The median age of the TRAs was 22 and the birth children, 26. The median age for the white adoptees was 25. Eighty-five percent of the TRAs and more than 90 percent of the birth children were not living in their parents' home. Locating them (with addresses and/or phone numbers in almost every one of the fifty states, plus some in the armed services and some living abroad) and arranging for personal interviews was extremely time-consuming and expensive. Thus, the fourth phase consisted of 4l black TRAs, 14 other TRAs—almost all of whom were Korean adoptees—13 white adoptees, and 30 birth children.

In 1983, we had asked the respondents to identify by race their three closest friends; 73 percent of the TRAs reported that their closest friend was white, and 71 and 62 percent said their second and third closest friends were white. Among the birth children, 89, 80, and 72 percent said their first, second, and third closest friends were white.

In 1991, 53 percent of the TRAs said their closest friend was white, and 70 percent said their second and third closest friends were white. For the birth children, more than 90 percent said their three closest friends were white. Comparison of the two sets of responses—those reported in 1983 and those given in 1991—show that the TRAs had shifted their close friendships from white to nonwhite and a higher percentage of the birth children respondents had moved into a white world.

The next portion of the interview focused on a comparison of the respondents' perceptions of their relationships with their parents at the present time and when they were living at home during adolescence; on their reactions to their childhood; and—for the TRAs—on how they felt about growing up in a white family.

Respondents' answers to the following questions are shown in table 4.5: "When you were an adolescent—and at the present time—how would you describe your relationship with your mother—and with your father?" The data indicate that, for the adopted as well as the birth children, relations with both parents improved between adolescence and young adulthood.

During adolescence, the TRAs had a more distant relationship with their mothers and fathers than did the birth children; but in the young adult years, more than 80 percent of both the TRAs and the birth children described their relationship to their mothers and their fathers as very or fairly close.

The respondents' ties to their siblings during adolescence, and currently, are shown in table 4.6. Not as dramatically as in their relationships with their parents—but in the same direction—the respondents' relationships with older or only siblings improved over time. For both the birth and the adopted children, a higher proportion reported that they had closer ties with their sibling at the present time than when they were adolescents. The pattern showing closer ties in the present with the second sibling holds for the birth children but not for the TRAs, although the large majority of respondents in both categories report close relationships with both their first and second siblings.

We asked the TRAs a series of questions about their relationships to family members during their childhood and adolescence, many of which focused on racial differences. The first such question was this:

Table 4.5   Relationships with Parents

How would you describe your relationship with your mother* during adolescence and at the present time?

Quality of Relationship	TRA		White Adopted		Birth	
	Adolescent	Present	Adolescent	Present	Adolescent	Present
Very close	29.1	45.5	—	61.5	43.3	50.0
Fairly close	32.7	43.6	53.8	15.4	33.3	30.0
Quite distant	14.5	1.8	23.0	23.0	6.7	6.7
Distant	23.6	5.5	23.0	—	16.7	6.7
No answer	—	3.6	—	—	—	13.3
	N = 55		N = 13		N = 30	

How would you describe your relationship with your father* during adolescence and at the present time?

Quality of Relationship	TRA		White Adopted		Birth	
	Adolescent	Present	Adolescent	Present	Adolescent	Present
Very close	30.9	43.6	7.7	38.5	43.3	36.7
Fairly close	34.5	38.2	61.5	53.8	30.0	43.3
Quite distant	14.5	3.6	23.0	23.0	3.3	6.7
Distant	18.2	10.9	15.4	—	20.0	10.0
No answer	1.8	3.6	—	—	3.3	3.3
	N = 55		N = 13		N = 30	

*For the adopted children, the term *adopted* mother and father was included in the question.

"Do you remember when you first realized that you looked different from your parents?," to which 75 percent answered that they did not remember. The others mentioned events such as "at family gatherings," "when my parents first came to school," "on vacations," "when we were doing out-of-the-ordinary activities," and "immediately, at the time of adoption." The latter response was made by children who were not infants at the time of their adoption.

That question was followed by this one: "How do you think the fact that you had a different racial background from your birth brother(s) and/or sister(s) affected your relationship with them as you were growing up?" Almost 90 percent of those who had siblings said it

Table 4.6   Relationships with Siblings

How would you describe your relationship with your (specific sibling, e.g., older, younger, brother, or sister specified) during adolescence and at the present time?

	Sibling #1					
Quality of Relationship	TRA		White Adopted		Birth	
	Adolescent	*Present*	*Adolescent*	*Present*	*Adolescent*	*Present*
Very close	27.3	30.9	7.7	38.5	46.7	43.3
Fairly close	30.9	43.6	69.2	38.5	36.7	43.3
Quite distant	18.2	10.9	—	—	10.0	3.3
Distant	20.0	12.7	15.4	15.4	6.7	10.0
Not app./ No answer	3.6	1.8	7.7	7.7	—	—

	Sibling #2					
Quality of Relationship	TRA*		White Adopted		Birth	
	Adolescent	*Present*	*Adolescent*	*Present*	*Adolescent*	*Present*
Very close	25.0	20.9	(Ns are too		20.0	30.0
Fairly close	45.4	48.8	small)		46.7	46.7
Quite distant	15.9	9.3			20.0	13.3
Distant	13.6	20.9			13.3	10.0

*Based on the 43 respondents who reported having a second sibling.

made little or no difference. The few others were divided among those who said that it had a positive effect, or a negative effect, or that they were not sure what, if any, effect it had.

We continued with this question: "Was being of a different race from your adoptive family easier or harder during various stages of your life?" Forty percent responded that they rarely found it difficult; 24 percent said the teen years were the most difficult; 22 percent found early childhood the most difficult; 8 percent said they found early childhood the easiest; and another 8 percent said they had a difficult time throughout their childhood and adolescence. Twenty-nine percent said that people of the same racial background as their own reacted "very negatively" or "negatively" toward them during their adolescence. The other responses ranged from "neutral" (37 percent) to "positive" (10 percent) and "very positive" (15 percent).

We asked the birth children how they felt about living in a family with black or other nonwhite siblings. Only one respondent reported "somewhat negative" feelings about having a sibling of a different race, and this same respondent felt that his parents had made a mistake in their decision to adopt a black child. Thirty percent acknowledged that there were times during their childhood when they felt out of place in their families—for example, when their families participated in "ethnic ceremonies" or attended black churches. But when asked, "How do you think being white by birth but having nonwhite siblings affected how you perceive yourself today?," all but 13 percent answered that the experience "had no effect." The others cited positive effects, such as "it broadened my understanding" and it "made me think of myself as part of the human race rather than of any special racial category."

Among those children whose parents lived in the same community, all of the TRAs and the birth children said they saw their parents at least two or three times a month; most children saw them almost every day or a couple of times a week.

On the 1983 survey, we asked the children a modified version of the following question: "If you had a serious personal problem (involving your marriage, your children, your health, and so on), who is the first person you would turn to; who is the next; who is the third?" Two other problems were posed: "If you had money problems" and "if you were in trouble with the law." In 1983, 46.8 percent of the TRAs chose a parent or a sibling; 45 percent of the birth children chose a parent or sibling; and 25 percent of the white adoptees chose a parent or a sibling.

In 1991—eight years later—when we again asked the children, "If you had a serious personal problem . . . ," we found no evidence that the TRAs were less integrated into their families than were the birth children. As shown in table 4.7, the TRAs were as likely, or more likely, to turn to parents and siblings as were the birth or white adopted children. But in almost all instances, the first persons that children in all three categories turned to were their adopted or birth parents. For the TRAs, a sibling was the next person. For the birth children, spouses and/or girlfriends or boyfriends constituted the second likely choice. The birth children and the white adoptees were older

Table 4.7 Persons Whom Respondents Would Approach with a Problem

Who are the first, second, and third persons you would seek out if you had a serious personal problem?

Persons	TRAs			White Adopted			Birth		
	1st	*2nd*	*3rd*	*1st*	*2nd*	*3rd*	*1st*	*2nd*	*3rd*
Parents	47.3	40.0	36.4	30.8	15.4	23.1	24.6	43.4	33.3
Siblings	9.1	23.6	—	23.1	30.8	7.7	3.3	20.0	13.3
Friends	29.1	27.3	32.7	23.1	30.8	14.4	23.3	26.7	33.3
Spouse/Boy/ girlfriends	12.7	5.4	3.6	7.7	7.7	23.1	46.6	3.3	6.7
Other	—	1.8	20.0	7.7	—	15.4	—	3.3	3.3
No answer	1.8	1.8	7.3	7.7	15.4	15.4	3.3	3.3	10.0

than the TRAs (median age twenty-six and twenty-five versus twenty-two), and this may explain their lesser likelihood to turn to their parents for help or advice.

Location of birth parents was another issue we raised again with the adopted children in the fourth phase of our study. In 1991, 75 percent said they had not tried to locate either of their birth parents. Among those who did make the effort, only one tried to locate a birth father; the others sought out their birth mothers. Of the fifteen TRAs who tried to locate their birth parents, seven were successful. Of those seven, three characterized their current relationship with their birth mothers as very or fairly close; the other four considered it somewhat or very distant. Thirteen of the fifteen asked for and obtained the help of their adopted parents in locating their birth mothers. The other two did not ask their adopted parents for help. Thus, over the years, most of the adopted children opted not to try to locate their birth parents. For the small minority who did, it did not turn out to be a wholly positive or special experience.

The last part of the interview focused on finding out how the TRAs felt about the practice of placing nonwhite—especially black—children in white homes, what recommendations they might have about adoption practices, and what advice they might have for white parents who are considering transracial adoption. We also asked the respondents to evaluate their own experiences with transracial adoption.

We opened the topic by stating, "You have probably heard of the position taken by the National Association of Black Social Workers and several councils of Native Americans strongly opposing transracial adoption. Do you agree or disagree with their position?" All of the respondents were aware of the NABSW's position. Eighty percent of the TRAs and 70 percent of the birth children said they disagreed with the NABSW position. Among the latter, 17 percent agreed and 13 percent were not sure. Only 5 percent of the TRAs agreed with the NABSW's position; the others were not sure how they felt about the issue. The reasons most often given for why they disagreed were that "racial differences are not crucial"; "TRA is the best practical alternative"; and "having a loving, secure relationship in a family setting is all important."

One black male adoptee said: "My parents have never been racist. They took shit for adopting two black kids. I'm proud of them for it. The Black Social Workers' Association promotes a separatist ideology."

Another black female commented: "It's a crock—it's just ridiculous. They [the NABSW] should be happy to get families for these children—period. My parents made sure we grew up in a racially diverse neighborhood. Now I am fully comfortable with who I am."

Another commented: "I feel lucky to have been adopted when I was very young [twenty-four days]. I was brought up to be self-confident—to be the best I can. I was raised in an honest environment."

In response to the question, "Would you urge social workers and adoption agencies to place nonwhite children in white homes?" Seventy percent of the TRAs and 67 percent of the birth children said yes without qualifications or stipulations. Almost all of the others placed some stipulations, the most common of which was that it should not be the placement of first choice—that a search should be made to find appropriate families of the same racial background as the children. The second most frequently mentioned stipulation was that the children should be placed with those white families who are "willing to make a commitment to exposing the child to his or her native culture."

We then shifted to a more personal note and asked, "How do you think being black (or, where appropriate, Korean or Native American) and raised by white parents has affected how you perceive yourself today?" One-third of the TRAs thought the adoption had a positive effect on their self-image. One-third thought it had no effect, and one-third did not know what effect the adoption had on their self-image.

One male adoptee said, "Multicultural attitudes develop better children. I was brought up without prejudice. The experience is fulfilling and enriching for parents and children."

Our next question was this: "All things considered, would you have preferred to have been adopted by parents whose racial background was the same as yours?" Seven percent said yes; 67 percent said no; 4 percent said they were not sure or did not know; and 22 percent did not answer. When asked why they held the position they did, most said, in essence, "My life has worked out very well"; "My parents love me"; and/or "Race is not that important."

One female black adoptee believed she "got the best of both worlds. I can be myself and have black and white friends. I don't look at people for their race."

Another said, "The transracial adoption experience gives us an open view of the world. Prejudice comes from ignorance."

When asked what advice they would give to parents who have the opportunity to adopt a young child of "your racial background" and about how she or he should be reared, 91 percent advised mostly that such parents be sensitive to racial issues; 9 percent advised that they reconsider.

One of the transracial adoptees who agrees with the position of the NABSW said, "I feel that I missed out on black culture. I can sit and read a book about Martin Luther King, but it is not the same." His advice to white parents who adopt black children is this: "Make sure they [the TRAs] have the influence of blacks in their lives; even if you have to go out and make friends with black families. It's a must—otherwise you are cheating them [the TRAs] of something valuable."

The last question we asked the TRAs was how they would describe their own racial backgrounds. Among the black TRAs, 32 percent answered black, and 68 percent said they were mixed (mostly black-white, a few black-Asians, and some black-Native Americans). Among the other TRAs, 5 percent described themselves as mixed, one as white, and others labeled themselves Native American, Korean, and Hispanic.

In the words of Elizabeth Bartholet:[22]

> The evidence from empirical studies indicates uniformly that transra-
> cial adoptees do as well on measures of psychological and social adjust-
> ment as black children raised inracially in relatively similar socio-eco-
> nomic circumstances. The evidence also indicates that transracial
> adoptees develop comparably strong senses of black identity. They see
> themselves as black and they think well of blackness. The difference is
> that they feel more comfortable with the white community than blacks
> raised inracially. This evidence provides no basis for concluding that,
> for the children involved, there are any problems inherent in transracial
> placement.

Finally, we include a few pieces of public opinion data, which show that when given the opportunity to express their views on transracial adoption most people, black and white, support it.

In the summer of 1997 the first national survey of public attitudes about adoptions and related policy issues was conducted by the Princeton Research Association. Among the questions included on the survey that was administered to 1,554 adults were these:

Do you approve or disapprove of a married couple who is white adopting a baby who is African American?

Do you approve or disapprove of a married couple who is African American adopting a baby who is white?

Eighty percent answered "approve" to the first question, and 77 percent answered "approve" to the second question.

A 1999 report published by the National Center for Health Statistics states that among a national sample of women currently seeking or planning to adopt, 51 percent of white women would prefer to adopt a white child, but 73 percent would accept a black child, and 89 percent would accept a child of another race. Among black women 52 percent would prefer a black child and 86 and 89 percent would accept a white child or a child of another race.

In January 1991, a *CBS This Morning* national poll asked 975 adults the following question: "Should race be a factor in adoption?" Seventy percent of white respondents said "no," and 71 percent of African Americans said "no." These percentages are the same as those reported by Gallup in 1971 when it asked a national sample the same question.

NOTES

1. Lucille J. Grow and Deborah Shapiro, *Black Children, White Parents: A Study of Transracial Adoption* (New York: Child Welfare League of America, 1974).

2. Joyce Ladner, *Mixed Families* (New York: Archer Press, Doubleday, 1977).

3. Ibid., pp. xii–xiii.

4. Ibid., pp. 255–256.

5. Charles H. Zastrow, *Outcome of Black Children-White Parents Transracial Adoptions* (San Francisco: R&E Research Associates, 1977).

6. Ibid., p. 81.

7. William Feigelman and Arnold Silverman, *Chosen Child: New Patterns of Adoptive Relationships* (New York: Praeger, 1983).

8. Womak and Fulton, "Transracial Adoption and the Black Preschool Child," *Journal American Academy of Child Psychiatry* 20 (1981): 712–724.

9. Ruth McRoy and Louis A. Zurcher, *Transracial and Inracial Adoptees* (Springfield, Ill.: Charles C. Thomas, 1983).

10. Ibid., p. 138.

11. Ibid., p. 138.

12. Joan Shireman and Penny Johnson, *Growing Up Adopted* (Chicago: Chicago Child Care Society, 1988).

13. Karen Vroegh, "Transracial Adoption: How It Is 17 Years Later," unpublished report, Chicago Child Care Society, Chicago, April 1992.

14. Richard P. Barth and Marian Berry, *Adoption and Disruption* (New York: Aldine de Gruyter, 1988), pp. 3–35.

15. Christopher Bagley, "Transracial Adoptions in Britain: A Follow-Up Study," *Child Welfare*, vol. 72, no. 3 (May–June 1993).

16. Ibid., p. 149.

17. David Brooks and Richard P. Barth, "Adult Transracial and Inracial Adoptees: Effects of Race, Gender, Adoptive Family Structure and Placement History on Adjustment Patterns," *American Journal of Orthopsychiatry*, vol. 69, no. 1 (January 1999): 87–99.

18. David Fanshel, *Far from the Reservation: The Transracial Adoption of American Indian Children* (Metuchen, N.J.: Scarecrow Press, 1972).

19. Ibid., p. 280.

20. Rita J. Simon, Howard Altstein, and Marygold S. Melli, *The Case for Transracial Adoption* (Washington, D.C.: American University Press, 1994), pp. 71–74.

21. Ibid., pp. 85–86.

22. Elizabeth Bartholet, "Where Do Black Children Belong? The Politics of Race Matching in Adoption," *University of Pennsylvania Law Review*, vol. 139 (1991): 1163.

APPENDIX A

The following is a summary of Transracial Adoption Studies published by the Stuart Foundation in their report "Adoption and Race: Implementing the Multiethnic Placement Act of 1994 and the Interethnic Adoption Provisions."

Table 4.A1   Transracial Adoption Studies

Study	Sample Characteristics	Major Findings
Bagley, C.	27 transracially adopted Afro-Caribbean and mixed-race children	No significant differences in measures of psychoneurosis, depression, and anxiety.
	25 inracially adopted Caucasian children	No significant differences in self-esteem, identity, or self-image.
		Majority of close friends of Black and mixed-race transracial adoptees are Caucasian.
		No significant differences in educational achievement.
Andujo, E.	30 transracially adopted Mexican-American children	No significant differences in self-concept.
	30 inracially adopted Mexican-American children	Transracial adoptees were more likely to identify selves as Americans, whereas inracial adoptees were more likely to

Study	Sample Characteristics	Major Findings
		identify selves as Mexican-American.
		Transracial adoptees were more highly acculturated and less connected to their culture than inracial adoptees.
		High-income inracial adoptees were also found to be highly acculturated and less connected to their culture, compared with medium- and low-income inracial adoptees.
McRoy, R. G., Zurcher, L. A. Lauderdale, M. L., & Anderson, R.	30 African-American transracial adoptees	No significant differences in self-esteem.
	30 African-American inracial adoptees	Significant differences in self-descriptions. Transracial adoptees were more likely than inracial adoptees to identify themselves as being adopted and to use racial self-referents.
		Significant differences in racial identity.
Simon, R. J., Altstein, H., & Melli, M. S.	1972—204 Caucasian adoptive families; 157 transracial adoptees; 42 inracial adoptees; and 167 birth children	1979—No difference among African-American transracial adoptees, other transracial adoptees, inracial adoptees, and birth children in findings on the family integration scale.
	1979—133 families	
	1984—96 families; 89 African-American transracial adoptees; 22 other transracial adoptees; 16 inracial adoptees; and 91 birth children	1984—No difference in self-esteem among groups.
		1991—No difference in family integration.
	1991—83 families; 41 African-American transracial adoptees; 14 other transracial adoptees; 13 inracial adoptees; and 30 birth children	
Rosenthal, J. A., Groze, V., Curel,	230 inracial adoptees—167 African-American; 25 Native Ameri-	Relationships between parent and child were significantly

Study	Sample Characteristics	Major Findings
II., & Westcott, P. A.	can; 15 Hispanic; and 23 bi- or multiracial 66 transracial adoptees—8 African-American; 5 Asian; 11 Native American; 20 Hispanic; and 22 bi- or multiracial	more positive in the inracial group. However, the differing characteristics at adoption appear primarily responsible for this difference.
Feigelman, W. & Silverman, A. R.	1977—737 Caucasian adoptive families 1981—372 families and children (47 African-American transracial adoptees; 181 Korean transracial adoptees; 19 Colombian transracial adoptees; 65 inracial adoptees; and 80 other adoptees)	1975—Adjustment of Caucasian and Colombian adoptees revealed no significant differences when the age of the adoptee and the age of placement were adjusted for. Age of the adoptee and age at placement were the only variables found significant. 1981—The only variable found to significantly affect adjustment in Caucasian and Colombian adoptees was the child's maladjustment score in 1975. Compared with Caucasian adoptees, African-American adoptees had significantly poorer adjustment. Age of adoptee at placement and the intensity of family and friends' opposition to adoption were the only variables found to be significant determinants of adjustment. 1981—Opposition to adoption and the adoptees maladjustment score in 1975 were the only significant determinants of adjustment. Korean adoptees were found to have better adjustment than Caucasian adoptees.
Brooks, D., & Barth, R. P.	242 Caucasian adoptive families—193 Asian transracial adoptees; 56 African-American	African-American males and Caucasian males experienced significantly more problem be-

Study	Sample Characteristics	Major Findings
	transracial adoptees; 87 Caucasian inracial adoptees	havior and poorer functioning than Asian females. Though not significant, they were also found to experience more problem behavior and poorer functioning than Asian males, African-American females, and Caucasian females.
		Family structure was the only variable found to significantly affect children's functioning. Specifically, being the only adopted child in a family containing one or more birth children increased the odds of the adopted child functioning poorly.
Vroegh, K. S.	1970—67 families (15 African American, 21 Caucasian, and 31 single parents), 118 African-American children 1992—55 families (no single parents), 15 transracial adoptees, 20 inracial adoptees	1992—Type of adoption (i.e., inracial vs. transracial) was not related to rate of adjustment. No significant differences in self-esteem. No significant differences in problem behavior.

5

✛

Results of Empirical Studies of Intercountry Adoptions

INTERCOUNTRY ADOPTION: A REVIEW OF EMPIRICAL RESEARCH

The following review of intercountry adoption (ICA) is limited to empirical investigations of issues such as quality of life, self-concept, racial/ethnic identity, and familial interaction found in referenced journals and as reported in such "national" newspapers as the *New York Times, Washington Post*, and *Wall Street Journal*. We will not refer to the myriad number of policy pieces or to emerging literature describing the health (incidence of tuberculosis, HIV/Hepatitis B and C, malaria, malnutrition, parasites, and so forth) and physiology (developmental delay, motor coordination, language acquisition, and so on) of intercountry adoptees. Nor will this review examine how intercountry adoptees adopted outside the United States and Canada are faring (e.g., Europe, Australia, and New Zealand).

Whether intercountry adoptions have been successful has only recently received serious scientific scrutiny. Several policy studies and a few empirical pieces did appear in the early 1970s and 1980s.[1] They were usually relatively limited anecdotal examinations restricted in scope and size to small samples, in most instances using case study designs.[2] In some circumstances investigations into limited aspects of intercountry adoption were part of a larger study.[3]

Pieces on ICA appeared in the medical literature in the late 1960s. For example, in 1967 and 1973 the American Academy of Pediatrics, in their publication *Adoption of Children,* reported that intercountry adoptees could suffer from such simple maladies as sleeping problems or from serious infectious diseases such as Hepatitis B and antibiotic-resistant tuberculosis.[4] In some instances, particularly if it were known that children were born to AIDS/HIV-positive mothers or had a history of hemophilia, it was recommended that children be screened for those diseases, especially those born in Brazil, Venezuela, Haiti, and Honduras.[5] The most recent article appearing in a medical journal was published in December 1998. It reported on the increased frequency with which family physicians were seeing intercountry adoptees in their practice and described some of the more common maladies found among these children.[6]

In one of the earliest empirical studies, D. S. Kim, in 1975 and 1976, examined 406 Korean children between twelve and seventeen years of age who were adopted by American families.[7] The research was conducted by the International Adoption Research Project at the University of Chicago and represented the first nationwide study of long-term adjustment by adopted Korean children. The major focus of the study was "to assess the identity and socialization patterns of teenage subjects." The study consisted of two groups: "Early group" children who were placed before they were one year of age and "later group" children who were placed at the age of six or older. The two groups were compared "in relation to the length of placement, transcultural factors, and family environment."

Quoting D. S. Kim:

> The study shows that adopted Korean children tend to progress very well in all areas of their lives, indicating no special problems in their overall, long-term adjustment. Their self-concept was remarkably similar to that of other American teenagers (represented by a norm group in a standard scale with an impressively positive self-esteem). Also, their assessment of various socialization processes appeared to be very healthy. . . . It is significant here to note that a warm and supportive

family environment was crucially important and responsible for positive outcomes.

But, Kim warned:

> With this positive evidence of progress and development, however, it should be recognized that these foreign children are still in the adolescent stage with an anticipatory socialization. It is questionable whether these positive indications will be maintained once they assume competitive adult roles in the larger society. There are some latent signs that seem to point to possible pathological symptomology among these children. For example, both sexes of adopted Korean children appeared to be extremely concerned with their physical appearance, complaining of their small stature, dark skin, flat noses, short legs, and so on. With this kind of negative body image, they tend to reject their own racial background. More than 25 percent of all the subjects in the study believed that they belonged to the "American" group, only a little more than 8 percent identified with the "Korean" group, and the rest identified with the "Korean-American" group. Actually, more than 60 percent of the subjects were, in fact, racially pure Korean.[8]

He went on to say:

> In fact, it is necessary for the child to be aware of personal heritage to develop his full potential or to define his place in society. Therefore, while avoiding ethnocentricity or reverse racism, foreign children can and should be instilled with a positive ethnic identity. Such a positive identity formation can furnish children a useful inclination to self-assertion, advocacy, and determination for their full socialization.[9]

In October 1987, the *Open Door Society News* reported a study conducted by Edward Suh, in which he spoke with (an unmentioned number of) families in Iowa who adopted Korean-born children. Parents reported that their children's main areas of difficulty lay in their language development, physical ailments, and disciplinary problems.[10]

In 1993, three relevant pieces (of which two were dissertations) appeared on various aspects of ICA. The first dissertation assessed how a group of forty-eight five-, six-, and seven-year-old Korean adoptees ethnically identified themselves by examining factors such as (adoptive) parents' interest in Korea, community demographics, adoptive family support-group membership with other families adopting Korean-born children, and so on. What the author found was very little covariance. Additional measures derived from interviewing the children, along with interpreting their reactions to puzzles and dolls, contributed little to clarifying a child's perception of his or her ethnic identity.[11]

In late 1993, John Politte completed a dissertation entitled, "Self-Esteem among Korean Adopted Pre-Adolescents."[12] His sample consisted of 41 families with 64 children, 51 Korean adoptees and 13 non-adopted siblings. The sample included 47 girls and 17 boys. All (except 4) were between the ages of eight and twelve. Politte measured variables traditionally used in this type of investigation—for example, self-esteem, school performance, conduct, and self-worth. He also spoke with parents and asked questions pertaining to their experiences as parents of racially different children, marital preferences for their children, and the extent to which they reinforced their child(ren)'s birth culture, racial perceptions, and so on.

Politte's results were consistent with previous findings in the literature. Intercountry adoptees did very well academically and scored especially high on measures of self-esteem and self-worth. Teasing a child about his or her Korean heritage did tend to minimally affect a child's self-concept and degree of social acceptance. Politte also found that the presence of another Korean adoptee in the family served to increase the scores of both on measures of social competence. Somewhat unclear was the effect on an adoptee's self-esteem of the parents' interest in having cultural artifacts in the home. No unusual results were found in the responses of the parents to Politte's questions regarding the previously described areas.

In April 1993, the General Accounting Office published a report entitled, "Intercountry Adoption: Procedures Are Reasonable, but Sometimes Inefficiently Administered."[13] One of the appendices indicated the responses of 203 families to the question: "Why did you choose intercountry adoption rather than domestic adoption?"[14] Table 5.1 describes the families' responses.

Table 5.1   Parents' Reasons for Choosing Intercountry Adoption

Why did you choose intercountry adoption rather than domestic adoption?	*Percent of Families**
Believed they were ineligible for domestic adoption	51
Believed intercountry adoption could be completed in less time than domestic adoption	38
Wanted to adopt a child with certain characteristics	27
Believed intercountry adoption would be easier than domestic adoption	20
Believed that intercountry adoption would cost less than domestic adoption	13
Were concerned about birth parent rights in domestic adoption	10
Wanted to help disadvantaged children	9
Were advised to pursue intercountry options	7
Had previous intercountry adoption experience	7
Believed there were no children available to adopt domestically	6

*N = 203 families. Families could indicate more than one reason.

The item receiving the highest score (51 percent of the families) was "believed they were ineligible for domestic adoption." The lowest response (6 percent of the families) saw parents believing that "there were no children available to adopt domestically." Both categories of responses reflect the extent to which our country has failed to educate the public about adoption. Without having the demographic specifics, one could guess that many of those who thought they were ineligible to adopt an American-born child were indeed eligible. Second, it is surprising that much of the public was and remains unaware that in excess of 50,000 U.S.-born children were (and are) available for adoption.

In 1994 the Search Institute published *Growing Up Adopted,* a major report describing the results of interviews with 715 families who adopted infants between 1974 and 1980.[15] When the survey was conducted in 1992–1993, the adoptees' ages ranged from 12 to 18. A total of 881 adopted children, 1,262 parents, and 78 nonadopted siblings participated in the study. Among the 881 adoptees, 289 were intercountry and/or transracially adopted, of which the largest single group was 199 Koreans, making up 23 percent of the total sample. (In addition to the Koreans, there were 27 African Americans [3 percent of the sample], 39 Hispanics [4 percent], and 24 Native Americans [3 percent] included in the study.)

The Search study reported that 81 percent of the "same race" adoptees and 84 percent of the TRAs (of whom 68 percent were Korean) said, "I'm glad my parents adopted me."

Various measures of mental health, self-esteem, and well-being were given to both inracial and transracial adoptees. The results are shown in tables 5.2, 5.3, and 5.4.

Table 5.5 reports the relative difficulties that transracial and intercountry adoptees had with their adoptions as compared against same-race adoptees. The large majority in all three categories report that adoption "has always been easy for me," and 5 percent and fewer report that it "has always been hard for me."

When asked, "Which has made growing up difficult for you: Your race, being adopted, both, or neither?" we see in table 5.6 that although intercountry adoptees report the least amount of difficulty in being adopted (2 percent), they had more difficulty with the racial differences between themselves and the rest of the world (35 percent as compared to 25 percent for all transracial adoptees).

Regarding attachment to their families, the study found, as shown in table 5.7, that transracial and intercountry adoptees are more likely than same-race adoptees to be attached to both parents.

When the data on parental responses were examined, some interesting findings emerged. For example, parents' perception of how emotionally attached their children are to them reveals that they rated

Table 5.2   Percent of Adolescents with High Self-Esteem

	Boys	Girls
National Sample[a]	51	39
All Transracial Adoptees	55	51
Asian TRAs[b]	53	53
Same-Race Adoptees	63	53

[a]National sample of public school adolescents; $N = 46,799$.
[b]In this study, transracial adoption is used in lieu of intercountry adoption.

Table 5.3 Four Measures of Psychological Health for Transracial and Same-Race Adoptions

Measure of Psychological Health	Range	Scale	Average	Scale Average in Comparison to Same-Race Group
Index of Well-Being	0–16	All TRA	11.23	No difference
		Asian	11.40	No difference
		Same-race	11.08	No difference
At-Risk Behavior	0–20	All TRA	1.80	No difference
		Asian	1.55	No difference
		Same-race	1.78	
Self-Rated Mental Health	1–5	All TRA	4.10	No difference
		Asian	4.07	No difference
		Same-race	4.11	
Achenbach	1–120	All TRA	44.63	No difference
		Asian	43.94	No difference
		Same-race	42.29	

their intercountry adoptees as having stronger attachments to them (46 percent) than all other transracial adoptees (42 percent) or inracially adopted adolescents (40 percent). Their perception of "very strong" attachments showed similar scores between intercountry and transracial adoptees (33 percent) but lowest scores (28 percent) for inracial adoptees.[16] Thus, the parents' perceptions of how emotionally attached they think their children are to them are not inconsistent with how the parents are in fact perceived by their children.

Except for the study conducted by the Search Institute, empirical examinations of intercountry adoptees continued to rely upon comparative small samples of less-than-adult-age adoptees, although with the passage of time adoptees' ages and sample sizes appear to be increasing.

In 1994 one of the authors of this work and his students analyzed a subset of twenty-nine Korean-born adult women adopted as infants.[17] The demographic variables examined included high school friendship and dating patterns, level of education, occupation, relationship with

Table 5.4   Racial Identity Among Transracially Adopted Adolescents

Items	Asian	African American	Hispanic	Native American	All TRA
			Percent Agree		
My parents want me to be proud of my racial background	79	87	83	81	79
Other people of my racial background accept me as one of them	51	65	63	52	54
My parent(s) try hard to help me be proud of my racial background	66	74	60	71	66
I wish I was a different race than I am	22	13	23	14	20
I wish my parent(s) were a different race	4	9	3	14	5
I get along better with people of my racial background	34	35	17	33	30
I feel more comfortable with people of my racial background than I do with other people	9	9	3	19	9
I get along equally well with people of my own racial background and people of other backgrounds	80	73	63	86	78
N	173	23	30	21	247

adoptive parents and siblings, religion and religiosity, race of spouse, if any, and so on. As a group, these women were satisfied with their lives, successful in their respective professions, and very glad they had been adopted by the families with whom they were placed.

In 1995 three articles were published on intercountry adoptees, ex-

Table 5.5   Relative Difficulty with Adoption

	Percent All TRAs	Percent Asian ICAs	Percent Same Race
Being adopted has always been easy for me	70	70	68
Being adopted used to be hard for me, but now it's easier	17	20	14
Being adopted used to be easy for me, but now it's harder	10	8	13
Being adopted has always been hard for me	4	2	5

amining issues such as acknowledgment of birth culture;[18] adolescent development issues;[19] and self-esteem, friendship patterns, and school achievement,[20] respectively. The latter research was based on a Canadian sample comparing 123 families having non-Canadian-born children with two cohorts: (1) Canadian-born adoptees and (2) birth children. The authors concluded that intercountry adoptees scored as high or higher than birth children on indicated measures but somewhat lower when compared to their siblings.

In 1996 the authors of "A Follow-Up Study of Adopted Children from Romania" investigated how a large group of Romanian adoptees, whose mean age is 4.6 years, are faring.[21] To no one's surprise, they found a relationship between length of time in an institution

Table 5.6   Difficulty Growing Up: Race versus Adoption

	All TRAs (%)	Asian ICAs (%)	Same Race (%)
My race	25	35	1
Being adopted	3	2	13
Both my race and adoption	12	12	2
Neither	59	52	83

Table 5.7   **Attachment to Families in Percent**

	All TRAs	*ICAs*	*Inracial*
I get along well with my parents	76	76	73
My mother accepts me as I am	85	87	81
My father accepts me as I am	85	87	78
There is a lot of love in my family	79	78	78
My parents often tell me they love me	83	86	82
I have lots of good conversations with my parents	61	65	67
My parents are easy to talk with	63	66	59

prior to adoption and post-adoption behavior. Generally, however, they report the adoptions as stable, with positive parent–child relationships.

The year 1998 witnessed several interesting empirical pieces that appeared in the literature, which examined various aspects of ICA. It has become increasingly apparent that heuristic interest in ICA is intensifying. In all likelihood this is a function of the large numbers of intercountry adoptees entering the United States each year and the fact that many are now approaching adolescence and early adulthood, a stage of development of considerable interest to social scientists. Because so many intercountry adoptees are nonwhite and are being raised in white families, they are receiving increased attention from social-psychological investigators.

In a study of 1,200 families who adopted children born in Eastern Europe, which appeared in the *Bulletin of the Joint Council on International Children's Services,* investigators found that the majority of the children were doing well in areas such as overall adjustment, attachment, emotional development, and health.[22]

The summer issue of the previously mentioned bulletin published another study of foreign-born children, adopted by 206 families. Here, too, authors reported that almost all intercountry adoptees had positive adjustment patterns (bonding and attachment).[23]

Generally supporting these conclusions was an investigation from Canada of 155 intercountry adoptees who reported that although they experienced racism and discrimination, they also felt very attached to their adoptive families. As a group, these adoptees had higher levels of self-esteem than their peers in the general population.[24]

An article presenting a somewhat less optimistic picture than the three noted previously appeared in the *Journal of Family Issues* early in 1998. Here, investigators found an association between the length of time children stayed in Romanian orphanages and parental difficulty in behavior management.[25]

As of 1998, most empirical research demonstrated that intercountry adoptees and their families generally adjust well to each other and that, by and large, adoptees are aware of and comfortable with their racial identities.

ADULT KOREAN ADOPTEES

This section presents a study conducted by the authors that describes the experiences of 124 white families all over the country who adopted 168 Korean children in the late 1960s and the 1970s. The major thrust of the report concerns the reactions that the currently adult Korean adoptees have to their Caucasian-American parents and siblings and to growing up in the United States. We gained access to these families by contacting the Holt Adoption Agency and asking them to help us locate families who had adopted at least one Korean child sixteen or more years ago. Over 85 percent of the families the Holt Agency was able to locate agreed to participate in the study. We then wrote or phoned the parents to arrange to interview both the parents and their adopted adult Korean children. Most of the parents were surveyed by mail; the children's interviews were conducted by phone.

Making only minor changes, we used the same parent and children questionnaires that we had used in the 1991 phase of the twenty-year Simon-Altstein study, except for substituting the appropriate racial background of the adoptees. The Korean "children's" questionnaire also included a few of the items asked of the TRAs in the 1983–1984 phase of the study.

The parents' questionnaire opened with this item:

> Think back, and with the knowledge of hindsight and the experiences you have accumulated, would you have done again what you did— adopt a child of a different race?

Ninety-five percent of the parents said "yes," they would have done what they did—adopt a child of a different race. Three percent were "not sure" and 2 percent said "no." When asked "Why?," over 80 percent of the parents who said they would do it again answered, "It was a positive, enriching, rewarding experience," "because he/she is our child and we love him/her," "he/she is like our birth child," and "every child needs a home." Among the five families who said "no" or that they "weren't sure," two sets of parents said they had adopted their children when he and she were nine and seven years old, and that the children had had traumatic experiences prior to being placed with them; two others cited pre-existing physical and emotional problems; and one family said "because we think our child would have been better off with a family of his own ethnic background."

We then asked:

> With all the thought and preparation that had gone into your decision, what about the experience surprised you the most?

The most frequent responses offered by over half of the respondents were: "There have been no major surprises"; "How easily our family and friends accepted our Korean son/daughter"; "How easy it was"; and "How quickly our child integrated/bonded with our family." Five percent of the families said the teen years were difficult, "particularly how much the child grappled with his/her identity."

Almost all of the parents said that the main impact that rearing a child of a different racial and cultural background had on their lives was that "it exposed us to a different culture," "to different groups of people that we either would not have known, or would not have known as well as we do"; "it broadened and enriched our lives"; "it made us more sensitive to racial issues, to what it means to be a minority"; "it made us more tolerant of different kinds of people, from all walks of life"; and "we saw that an adopted child is no different than a biological child."

Finally, we asked the parents:

Would you recommend that other families like your own adopt a child of a different race or culture?

Ninety percent answered "yes," they would recommend that other families like their own adopt a child of a different race. One percent said they would not, and 9 percent were not sure whether they would recommend transracial adoptions to other families similar to their own. Those who would recommend it said they would also tell the parents to love the child as if it had been born to them, to be aware that the child comes from a different culture and try to expose him or her to that culture, and to generally be aware of the responsibility they are taking on.

We turn now to the adoptees' responses.

Ninety-four percent of the 168 children were born in Korea, about half were born in Seoul, and the others came from Vietnam, India, Bangladesh, and Thailand. Thirty-eight percent were brought to the United States before they were one year old. Another 27 percent came before they were two years old, and 80 percent arrived before their fourth birthdays. At the time they were interviewed, 4 percent were still attending high school. The educational attainments of the others are described in table 5.8.

In two-thirds of the families, the parents have paid or are fully or partially paying their children's tuition, room and board, and other university expenses.

Almost all of the respondents reported living in their parents' home until they went off to school, married, or went to work full time. Two percent said they left because they were not getting along with their parents. Among those currently employed full time, the occupational distribution is described in table 5.9.

Thirty-six percent of the respondents were married at the time the

Table 5.8   Highest Degree Obtained Thus Far by Percent

High School Diploma	53
A.A. Degree	8
B.A./B.S.	24
M.A./M.S./M.B.A.	3
M.D.	1
Ph.D.	1
Other/N.A.	6*
N	168

*Only one respondent reported that he did not complete high school.

interviews were conducted, none to a Korean. Seventy-seven percent are married to Caucasians, 8 percent to American blacks, and 15 percent to Hispanics and others. Twenty-four percent have children; four of the respondents adopted at least one child, and one of the adopted children is Korean.

The next section of the interview probed the ties the respondents have to the country in which they were born and from which most of them were adopted before they were two years old. Only one in five of the respondents reported having visited Korea. Among those who did, twelve went on a Holt Agency–sponsored "Motherland Tour," nine went with their parents or a sibling, five went alone, and the other eleven went with a spouse, a friend, or via the U.S. Navy. Although only 20 percent reported having visited Korea, two-thirds said they had artifacts, books, photos, and so forth, in their homes that describe some aspect of Korean society. But as the responses in table 5.10 indicate, the large majority can neither speak, read, nor write Korean.

When asked to describe the racial/ethnic characteristics of their

Table 5.9   Occupational Categories by Percent

Professional	25
Administrative/Clerical	20
Service	20
Skilled/Laborer	7
Unemployed	12
Other	16

Table 5.10 Korean Language Facility

	Percent Speaking	Percent Reading	Percent Writing
Fluently	0.0	1.8	1.8
Fairly fluently	2.4	3.0	3.0
Hardly at all	13.7	5.4	5.9
Not at all	83.9	89.9	89.3

three closest friends, when they were in high school and "now" (at the time of the interview), at least 80 percent of the respondents reported having white friends.

In response to questions about the types of people they dated when they were in high school, 72 percent answered "white American," 9 percent said "mainly whites, some blacks and other minorities," and 4 percent answered "Asians." Fifteen percent said they did not date in high school. In response to the follow-up question, which was "Why did you choose to date the people you did?," 52 percent said, "They were the people I was most attracted to on the basis of looks, common interests, and personality." Most of the others said their school was predominantly white and there were "few other dating options."

Next we turned to a more detailed analysis of the respondents' memories and perceptions of their childhood. We started by asking: "In thinking back about your childhood, what were the most positive aspects about it?," followed by "What were the most negative aspects about it?" For the positive side, 68 percent said, "growing up in a warm, loving family," 30 percent said "having lots of friends," and 21 percent said "being afforded a wide variety of educational and other opportunities." Nine percent said "doing well in sports."

For the most negative aspects, 17 percent said they had none or so few they could not describe them. No one said that in response to the question about the positive aspects of their childhood. The categories of negative experiences most frequently cited are listed in table 5.11.

Continuing to probe about their childhood, we then asked:

When you were a child, how did you feel about having a different racial and ethnic background than your parents?

Table 5.11   Negative Experiences Most Frequently Cited

	Percent
Difficulties getting along with my adoptive mother	19
Experiences I had related to racial prejudice	14
Difficulties getting along with my adoptive father	12
Difficulties getting along with my peers at school	11

Do you remember when you first realized that you "looked" different than your parents?

For those who had siblings born to their adoptive parents, we asked:

How do you think the fact that you had a different racial/ethnic background affected your relationships with your brother(s) and/or sister(s)?

Was being of a different race and ethnicity than your adoptive family easier or harder during various stages of your life (e.g., during childhood, adolescence, etc.)?

How did people who were of the same ethnic background as you react to you when you were an adolescent?

Aside from the obvious racial/ethnic differences, did you ever feel that somehow you just did not fit in with your adoptive family; that your temperament and/or personality were different from other family members? If you did, please explain under what conditions, or in what situations they occurred.

Finally:

Did you ever attribute these differences between you and your adopted parents to the fact that in some way, from what you know, you were behaving like either of your birth parents?

Now for the responses! Sixty-four percent of the respondents said, "It simply did not matter that my parents were of a different racial background than I was." Fifteen percent thought of it as having "positive" aspects, and 12 percent saw some negative aspects to the differences. Only 39 percent remembered when they first realized that they looked different than their parents. Almost half of those who remembered said, "Immediately, as soon as I was adopted." They had all been adopted when they were at least four years old.

Like the responses to the item about being of a different race than their parents, most of the respondents said about being of a different race than their sibling(s), "it made little or no difference." Six percent viewed it as positive, and 9 percent viewed it negatively. As for which periods in their lives being of a different race was easier or harder, almost half (48 percent) of the respondents said they just didn't think about it and could not designate an easier or harder time at any stage of their lives. Ten percent said they had difficult periods throughout both childhood and adolescence, 24 percent said adolescence was the most difficult, and 13 percent said early childhood was the most difficult. Four percent said early childhood was the easiest, and 1 percent said adolescence was the easiest.

Only 38 percent could answer the question "How did people who were of the same ethnic background as you react to you when you were an adolescent?," because the others said they encountered "very few or no" Koreans during their childhood and adolescence. Of those who answered, 17 percent said, "It didn't seem to matter to them." Eighteen percent said they responded positively, and 12 percent said the responses were usually negative.

Seventy percent said that they "never" felt that they did not fit into their adopted family (for whatever reasons, e.g., temperament, personality, etc.). Among the 30 percent who did report such feelings, the most typical explanations were "I was much louder and more expressive than other people in my family"; "I was quieter and more introspective"; "I related to people differently"; and "I had different interests." None of the explanations were shared by more than 5 percent of the respondents. But even among those who noticed differences between themselves and other family members, practically no adoptees attributed the difference to the possibility that their own behavior was similar to that of their birth parents, in part because hardly any of them had known or knew anything about their birth parents.

The next section examined the respondents' accounts of their current relationships with their parents and siblings. We first asked whether they lived in the same communities as their parents and found that 38 percent did. Of those who did not, 55 percent lived within 200 miles of their parents. Among those who were not living at home, 25 percent said they see their parents at least once a week, 30 percent at least once a month, and the others said several times a year. Sixty-two percent reported talking with them on the phone at least once a week and 27 percent said at least once a month. None of the respondents reported no contacts with their parents; two reported visits once every other year, and one every two to three years.

Table 5.12 describes the responses to these questions:

How would you describe your relationship at the present time with your adopted mother/father?

When you were an adolescent, how would you describe your relationship with your adopted mother/father?

The responses show that relationships had been close with both parents during adolescence and had gotten closer as the children became adults. Only 13 percent perceived their current relationship with either their mother or their father to be "quite distant" or "distant." When we asked those respondents who had answered "quite distant" or "distant" to explain why they were not close to their parent(s),

Table 5.12   Quality of Relationship with Parents in Percent

Quality of Relationship	Mother		Father	
	Adolescent	*Present*	*Adolescent*	*Present*
Very close	40.1	50.0	36.9	43.5
Fairly close	31.8	35.1	41.1	35.1
Quite distant	14.7	6.0	4.8	3.0
Distant	12.4	7.1	14.9	10.1
No Answer/Other*	1.2	1.8	2.4	8.3

*Three of the fathers had died when the respondents were adolescents and twelve of the fathers were deceased at the time the interviews were conducted.

most of the respondents said of their mother, "She doesn't accept the kind of person I am," "She doesn't approve of my lifestyle," and "She objects to my friends." About their fathers, more of them put the blame on the parent: for example, "He has a substance abuse problem"; "He is non-verbal," "unaffectionate," or "irresponsible." But those descriptions fit less than 15 percent of either the mothers or the fathers.

For those who told us that the relationship between them and their parents had changed from the time they were adolescents until now, we asked, "Why?" Most answered that there was a "natural break when I went off to college." Others cited different interests, and some cited changes in the family (e.g., deaths of fathers, divorces, illnesses) that brought parents and children closer.

Another way of assessing how close the respondents feel toward their adopted families is by examining their responses to the following question:

> If you had a serious personal problem involving, for example, your marriage, your children, your health, etc., who are the three people you would most likely turn to for help or advice?

We also asked the same questions, "If you had a serious money problem . . . ?" and "If you were in trouble with the law . . . ?" The results shown in table 5.13 clearly indicate that almost all the respondents—between 93 and 99 percent—would turn to their parents as one of the three sources. Friends are the next most frequently cited category, especially for a "personal problem," followed by a sibling.

Table 5.13   Type of Problem in Percent

Category of Person	Personal	Money	Law
Parent(s)	99.3	95.3	92.6
Friend(s)	73.0	41.9	52.7
Sibling(s)	48.0	34.0	40.0
Spouse/Boyfriend/Girlfriend	6.0	20.9	11.5
Other Relatives (Grandparents, Aunts, Uncles)	30.4	18.9	25.7
Other	30.4	18.9	25.7
No One	2.0	0.7	—

It is worth noting that, within the "parents" category, mothers were consistently cited more often than fathers.

The last part of the interview focused on policy issues concerning transracial adoption. We began by asking:

> Would you urge social workers and adoption agencies to place Hispanic, Korean, Asian, black, or other nonwhite children in white homes?

Eighty-seven percent said "yes," 9 percent said "no," and 3 percent said they "weren't sure." We followed up with, "If 'no,' please explain why not," and "If 'yes,' would you make any stipulations in that policy?" Among the 10 percent who opposed the practice, almost all of them said, "Race and ethnicity are very important," and "Whites simply cannot understand what it means to be Asian." For the 87 percent who said "yes," they would urge adoption agencies to make transracial placements, about half made no stipulations. The others made comments such as "Yes, only if the adoptive parents are willing to make a commitment to expose the child to her native culture" and "Yes, such children should be placed in white homes only after an exhaustive search has been made to try to place the child in a home of her own racial/ethnic background." Others urged having the families live in multi-racial neighborhoods. Most of the other stipulations focused on the importance of a "stable, loving family," "adopt when the children are very young," and "families may need counseling."

In response to the question: "How do you think being Korean by birth but reared by white parents has affected how you perceive yourself today?" One-third said, "It had no effect on my self-image one way or the other." Another third said, "It had a positive effect on my self-image" and "It broadened my view of different races." Thirteen percent stated that it had a negative effect on their self-image and an additional 5 percent said, "I feel like a banana."[26] The other 15 percent gave a range of "other" explanations.

For those respondents who were married at the time of the interview (one-third, and only one to a Korean), we asked: "How important was the racial or ethnic background of your spouse in your decision to marry?" Eighty percent said, "It did not matter." Most of the others said, in essence, "I cared more about personal characteristics than race." Although 22 percent have children, half of them were too young for the respondent to answer "How does your child identify his/her racial background?" Among the seventeen respondents who did answer, nine described some combination of "Korean," or "Asian/white," or "American."

When asked, "How would you describe yourself (focusing on racial/ethnic background)?" 30 percent answered, "Korean"; 32 percent said, "Korean/Asian-American"; 5 percent, "Asian"; 20 percent said, "American"; 7 percent said, "White"; and the other 6 percent said Amerasian, Indian, Thai, and so forth. For some 73 percent of the respondents, their Korean-Asian heritage is very much part of their current identity.

The last two items in the formal interview asked:

All things considered, would you have preferred to have been adopted by parents whose racial and ethnic background was the same as yours? If so, please explain why.

The responses are shown in table 5.14.

For those who answered "no," the explanations were mainly that "everything worked out well for me," "race should not be that important," and "my parents loved me."

And finally:

What advice would you give to white parents who have the opportunity to adopt a young child of your racial background about how he/she should be reared?

Table 5.14   Percent Preference for Adoption by Same Race Parent

No	80
Yes	7
Don't know	5
No answer	8

The responses fell into two major categories. One emphasized "Just do it" and "Be sure you love that child and treat him as yours." The other emphasized that parents "must be sensitive to racial issues," "show respect for his/her culture," "talk about her/his background," and "live in a mixed neighborhood."

The overall impressions that emerge from these interviews are that Korean transracial adoptees are aware of their backgrounds but are not particularly interested in making them the center of their lives. They feel good about having grown up with the families they did. They are committed to maintaining close ties with their adopted families and are supportive of policies that promote transracial adoptions.

NOTES

1. Joe, p. 7; Eugenie Hochfield, "Across National Boundaries," *Juvenile Court Judge Journal* 14 (October 1963): 3–7; Burton Sokoloff, Jean Carlin, and Hien Pham, "A Five Year Follow-Up of Vietnamese Refugee Children," *Clinical Pediatrics* 23 (October 1984): 565–570; S. Peter Kim, "Behavioral Symptoms in 3 Transracially Adopted Asian Children: Diagnosis Dilemma," *Child Welfare* 59 (1980): 213–224; Jerri Ann Jenista and Daniel Chapman, "Medical Problems of Foreign Born Adopted Children," *American Journal of Diseases of Children* 141 (March 1987): 298–302; Committee on Adoptions, American Academy of Pediatrics, *Adoption of Children*, 2d ed. (1967), p. 69; Committee on Adoptions and Dependent Care, American Academy of Pediatrics, *Adoption of Children*, 3d ed. (1973), p. 72.

2. Dong Soo Kim, "How They Fared in American Homes: A Follow-Up Study of Korean Children in the U.S.," *Children Today* 6 (March/April 1977): 2–6; Dong Soo Kim, "Issues in Transracial and Transcultural Adoption," *Social Casework* 59 (1978): 477–486; Cliff Picton, "Post Adoption Support," *Adoption and Fostering* 88 (1977): 21–25; S. Peter Kim, Sungdo Hong, and Bok Soon Kim, "Adoption of Korean Children by New York Area Couples: A Preliminary Study," *Child Welfare* 8 (1979): 419–427; Glenda French, "Intercountry Adoption: Helping a Young Child Deal with Loss," *Child Welfare* 65 (May–June 1986): 272–279; Hei Sook Park Wilkinson, *Birth Is More than Once: The Inner World of Adopted Korean Children* (Bloomfield, Mich.: Sunrise Ventures, 1985).

3. William Feigelman and Allan Silverman, *Chosen Children: New Patterns of Adoptive Relationships* (New York: Praeger, 1983). For a particularly useful annotated bibliography, see Lois Ruskai Melina, *Adoption, an Annotated Bibliography and Guide* (New York: Garland Publishing, 1987).

4. American Academy of Pediatrics, *Adoption of Children*, 2d ed. (1967), p. 60; 3d ed. (1973), p. 72.

5. Jerri Ann Jenista and Daniel Chapman, "Medical Problems of Foreign Born Adopted Children," *American Journal of Diseases of Children* 141 (March 1987): 298–302; Margaret Hostetter and Dana E. Johnson, "International Adoption: An Introduction for Physicians," *American Journal of Diseases of Children* 143 (March 1989): 325–332.

6. Christopher S. Quarles and Jeffrey H. Brodie, "Primary Care of International Adoptees," *American Family Physician,* vol. 58, no. 9 (December 1998): 2025. I would like to thank Dr. Samuel Altstein for bringing this article to my attention.

7. D. S. Kim, "Intercountry Adoptions: A Study of Self-Concept of Adolescent Korean Children Who Were Adopted by American Families," unpublished Ph.D. thesis, University of Chicago, 1976.

8. Ibid., p. 56.

9. Ibid., p. 84.

10. Edward Suh, "Life Adjustment Problems among Adopted Korean Children," *Open Door Society News* (October 1987): 3.

11. Jill C. Cole, "Perceptions of Ethnic Identity among Korean Born Adoptees and Their Caucasian-American Parents," *Dissertation Abstracts International-A,* vol. 54, no. 1 (July 1993): 317. University Microfilms, #9504358, also cited in *FACE FACTS,* (July/August 1995): 24–26. Kevin Lee Wickes, "Transracial Adoption: Cultural Identity and Self-Concept of Korean Adoptees," *Dissertation Abstracts International-B,* vol. 54, no. 8 (February 1994): 4374. University Microfilms, #9504358, also cited in *FACE FACTS* (July/August 1995): 24–26. Kevin Lee Wickes, "Transracial Adoption: Cultural Identity and Self-Concept of Korean Adoptees," *Dissertation Abstracts International-B,* vol. 54, no. 8 (February 1994): 4374.

12. John Politte, "Self Esteem Among Korean Adopted Pre-Adolescents," University Microfilms, #9504358, 1993.

13. "Intercountry Adoption: Procedures Are Reasonable, but Sometimes Inefficiently Administered," GAO/NSIAD-93-83.

14. Ibid., no. 17, p. 59.

15. Peter L. Benson, Anu R. Sharma, and Eugene C. Roehlkepartain,

"Growing Up Adopted: A Portrait of Adolescents and Their Families," Search Institute, Minneapolis, Minn. (June 1994).

16. Ibid., p. 99; op. cit., no. 20, p. 109; op. cit., no. 20, p. 107; op. cit., no. 20, p. 103.

17. Howard Altstein, "Clinical Observations of Adult Intercountry Adoptees and Their Adoptive Families," *Child Welfare*, vol. 73, no. 3 (May–June 1994): 261.

18. Barbara C. Trolley, Julia Wallin, and James Hansen, "International Adoption: Issues of Acknowledgment of Adoption and Birth Culture," *Child and Adolescent Social Work*, vol. 12, no. 6 (December 1995): 465–479.

19. Frank C. Verhulst, Bieman den Versluis, and J. M. Herma, "Developmental Course of Problem Behavior in Adolescent Adoptees," *Journal of the American Academy of Child and Adolescent Psychiatry*, vol. 34, no. 2 (February 1995): 151–159.

20. Joyce S. Cohen and Anne Westhues, "A Comparison of Self-Esteem, School Achievement and Friends between Intercountry Adoptees and Their Siblings," *Early Child Development and Care* 106 (February 1995): 205–224.

21. Victor Groze and Daniela Ileana, "A Follow-Up Study of Adopted Children from Romania," *Child and Adolescent Social Work*, vol. 13, no. 6 (December 1996): 541–565. Robert S. Bausch and Richard T. Serpe, "Negative Outcomes of Interethnic Adoption of Mexican American Children," *Social Work*, vol. 42, no. 2 (March 1997): 136–143.

22. Mary Essley and Linda Perilstein, "Eastern European Adoptions," *Bulletin of the Joint Council on International Children's Services* (Spring 1998): 8; and http://www.cradlehope.org/survey/html.

23. D. Clauss and S. Baxter, "Rainbow House International Survey of Russian and Eastern European Children," *Bulletin of the Joint Council on International Children's Services* (Summer 1998): 6.

24. Anne Westhues and Joyce S. Cohen, "The Adjustment of Intercountry Adoptees in Canada," *Children and Youth Services Review*, vol. 20, nos. 1–2 (1998): 115–134.

25. Henry Mainemer, Lorraine C. Gilman, and Elinor W. Ames, "Parenting Stress in Families Adopting Children from Romanian Orphanages," *Journal of Family Issues*, vol. 19, no. 2 (March 1998): 64–80.

26. Spokespersons for the National Association of Black Social Workers have dubbed black children adopted by white families "oreos," i.e., black on the outside with white psyches. The "banana" simile evokes the same image for Korean transracial adoptees.

APPENDIX B

Media Accounts of Intercountry Adoptions

One measure of an event's significance is the extent to which it captures the attention of the mass media. Most people would imagine that intercountry adoption, affecting only a small fraction of the U.S. population, would not be so contentious an issue as to generate as much attention as it does. Instead, we find that stories about ICA appear in our nation's newspapers and other mass media outlets with considerable frequency. For example, within a few weeks during the period we were writing this book, stories appeared about adoptions from the former Soviet Republic of Georgia; Russia; Eastern Europe; China; Romania; and Central America.

On a page 1 story in the *New York Times*, entitled "Hands Off Our Babies, a Georgian Tells America,"[1] American adoption agencies were warned by Mrs. Nanuli Shevardnadze, wife of Eduard Shevardnadze, president of the former Soviet Republic of Georgia, not to attempt to remove orphaned children from Georgia to the United States. She is quoted in the article as saying:

> I am categorically against foreign adoption. Our nation's gene pool is being depleted. All the Georgian people are suffering hardships. Let our children suffer, too.

Mrs. Shevardnadze implied that her husband shared her views.

To place these remarks in context, Eduard Shevardnadze had a scheduled meeting with President Clinton in Washington three weeks after the previously mentioned comments were made. Indeed, the day Mr. Shevardnadze arrived to meet with President Clinton, the *New York Times* reported that: ". . . one of the first questions he may face is about the fate of a dozen Georgian orphans whom American families are struggling to adopt."[2]

In speaking about the visit, the Georgian ambassador to the United States said: "I am afraid that foreign adoptions will become the issue of his visit."[3]

The remarks of Mrs. Shevardnadze were not atypical of other statements and allegations from those opposing foreign adoptions. At the extreme are stubborn accusations that children, under the guise of being adopted in the West, are in reality sent here for their internal organs ("baby parts") to be used in transplants. These allegations were also heard in relation to foreign adoption from Georgia.[4] Although these charges have been investigated over the years by various governmental and nongovernmental organizations in both the United States and other countries with no substantiation, they persist.[5]

Another story that received wide coverage in the media appeared a month prior to the Georgian events, in May 1997. An American couple returning home from Russia, after adopting two four-year-old Russian girls, was accused of in-flight child abuse.[6] Upon landing in New York, the adoptive couple was arrested and charged with third-degree assault, second-degree harassment, and endangering the welfare of children. The interaction between the adoptive parents and children was such that several passengers voluntarily missed their connecting flights in order to substantiate the alleged abuse.[7] The children were removed from their adoptive parents and placed into New York City's foster care system.[8] A custody trial began shortly thereafter.[9]

The children were then moved to Arizona, their adoptive parents' home state, where they were once again placed with a foster family. By November, six months after they arrived in the United States, they were still in foster care, with their fifth foster family (their adoptive mother's brother), two in New York and three in Arizona. In a New York trial, the adoptive parents were convicted on six counts of neglect and allowed only supervised visits.[10] In December, the court ordered the parents into couples therapy and psychotherapy with their adopted daughters. The judge also allowed unsupervised weekend visits. At that time it was hoped that by March 1998, ten months after their adoption, the adoptive parents would be able to have physical custody of their adopted children.[11] Indeed, in a trial held on February 23, the adoptive parents were granted absolute custody of their two adopted daughters. Custody, however, was contingent upon monthly progress reports to be submitted to the court, the parents remaining in therapy, and power given to Arizona child welfare authorities to make unscheduled visits to their home.[12] Thus ended a saga that began in May 1997, which for a time saw the threat of the Russian Duma passing legislation that would reduce or eliminate all Russian adoptions to the United States. The by now five-year-old girls had been in five separate foster homes.

A second Russian adoption receiving wide media attention involved the death of the adoptee.[13] Specifically, the adoptive mother was found guilty of child abuse resulting in death and was sentenced to twenty-two years in prison. The defense claimed that the adoptee suffered from "reactive attachment disorder," a *DSM-IV* diagnosis characterized by a child's inability to bond with a parent, combined with uncontrollable tantrums often accompanied by self-mutilation. Early emotional deprivation is given by most as the cause of these behaviors.[14] The child in question was adopted just shy of his third birthday, having spent practically all of his life in a Russian orphanage. The adoptive mother argued the child died of self-inflicted injuries as a result of his psychiatric disorder.

Many people saw a connection between the previously described well-publicized events and Russia's parliament drafting, in late November 1997, of new and much more restrictive regulations governing adoption of Russian children by non-Russians, especially Americans.[15] Should Russia be eliminated as a source of adoptable children, American families would surely feel its effect. Estimates vary widely from 190,000[16] to 533,000[17] as to the number of children housed in Russia's baby houses and orphanages. Many of these children are not currently free for adoption but may become so in the future. In 1996 Russian domestic adoptions accounted for some 9,000 children, a fraction of the number of children available for adoption.[18] Were Russia to end all adoptions to Americans or even significantly curtail adoptions, a potentially enormous reservoir of children would be eliminated.

One important reason adoptions from Russia (and Romania as well) may be especially problematic is that, on the average, Russian adoptees tend to be older than adoptees from other countries. Age at time of adoption has long been considered a leading cause of post-adoption difficulties. The latter is primarily due to the neglect and sometimes abuse these children suffered while in orphanages.[19] A study published in November 1997 of Romanian children adopted by Canadian parents again demonstrated the noxious mix of length of time spent in an orphanage and age at adoption. In comparing three groups of Canadian children: (category 1) [46] nonadopted Canadian-born children; (category 2) [29] Romanian children adopted before the age of four months; and (category 3) [46] Romanian children who spent from eight months to four and a half years in Romanian orphanages, and were on the average one-and-a-half-years-old at the time of adoption, the author found that 35 percent of "category three" children had one or two of the following psychosocial difficulties:

an IQ of less than 85
insecure attachments (found in only 5 percent of all
North American children)
stereotypical behaviors (e.g., rocking)
behavior problems warranting professional intervention

Thirty percent had three or four of the previous problems. Thirty-five percent did not exhibit any of the problems.[20]

Yet another ICA issue receiving attention involves the rise in the number of Chinese orphans (almost exclusively females) adopted by U.S. citizens. During the summer of 1997, the *New York Times* ran almost back-to-back page 1 articles on China's one child policy and, in a second seemingly unrelated article, on the increase in foreign adoption of children born in China.[21] Although the *Times* did not connect the two pieces, the argument has long been made that a primary reason for China's willingness to allow some of its female infants to be adopted by foreigners is directly connected to its 1979 policy of allowing each Chinese family to have (e.g., keep) only one child. When that infant is female, because of the ancient custom of valuing male over female children it is likely that the family will place her for adoption or, far worse, simply abandon or kill her with the hope that their next child will be male. Some suggest that female Chinese children are being eliminated "on a massive scale."[22] Many families repeatedly relinquish female infants until a male is born. By 1997 this has led to China's having a "surplus population" of female orphans. In New York City alone, in 1997 there were close to 1,000 Chinese adoptions of females under the age of five.

As 1998 progressed, ICA once again began to draw the public's attention. In April the *Washington Post* ran a story reporting that since 1987 a Louisiana adoption agency has been bringing pregnant Russian women into the United States to deliver their children, only to immediately surrender them for adoption to American families. Children born in the United States are automatically U.S. citizens, and adoptive parents are spared having to deal with the at times Byzantine regulations governing adoption outside the United States, especially in Russia. The Immigration and Naturalization Service said it was beginning a criminal investigation into the allegations.[23]

In May 1998, the *New York Times Magazine* ran a cover story entitled "Attachment Theory: The Ultimate Experiment."[24] Citing primarily Romanian orphans and the deplorable conditions in most Romanian orphanages as examples, the author (Margaret Talbot) delved into the often-catastrophic effects of early and prolonged emotional deprivation on these children. The article describes the traumatic experiences of American families who have adopted some 18,000 primarily Romanian orphans (and, to a lesser extent, others from Eastern Europe) and their struggles in attempting to cope with these children's behaviors. The piece paints a bleak picture of East European adoption, especially from Romania.

Finally, the machinations and deceptions inherent in some adoptions from Central America, especially those from Honduras and Guatemala, are revealed in a piece appearing in the *Baltimore Sun*.[25] The article describes various ways "baby brokering" attorneys in Guatemala employ deception to illegally remove infants from their poor and illiterate birth mothers. These infants are then provided to foreign couples for adoption, usually in the United States. Taken as a whole, the previously mentioned pieces appearing in some of America's leading publications do not present an altogether positive picture of ICA.

NOTES

1. Alessandra Stanley, "Hands Off Our Babies, a Georgian Tells America," *New York Times,* June 29, 1997, p. 1.

2. Alessandra Stanley, "Issue of Foreign Adoption Follows Shevardnadze to Washington," *New York Times,* July 16, 1997, p. A5.

3. Ibid.

4. Roger Morris, "Toward a Policy That's No Longer Foreign," *New York Times*, February 4, 1992, Op-Ed.

5. "Traffic in Baby Parts Has No Factual Basis," Letter to the Editor, *New York Times*, February 26, 1992, p. 20.

6. Norimitsu Onishi, "Couple Accused of Abuse of Two Newly Adopted Girls," *New York Times*, May 30, 1997, p. A28.

7. "Couple Has Supervised Visit with Adopted Russian Girls," no author, *Baltimore Sun*, June 11, 1997, p. 2; Katharine Q. Seelye, "Custody Trial Opens for 3 Adopted Children Hit on Plane," *New York Times*, July 3, 1997, p. A21; Katharine Q. Seelye, "Couple Struck Adopted Girls on Flight, Passengers Testify," *New York Times*, October 7, 1997, p. 27.

8. "Legal Limbo in Adoption Case," no author, *New York Times*, June 17, 1997, p. A7.

9. Op. cit., Seelye, July 3, 1997, p. 7.

10. Katharine Q. Seelye, "Couple Struck Adopted Girls on Flight, Passengers Testify," *New York Times*, October 7, 1997, p. 27; Katharine Q. Seelye, "Couple Accused of Beating Russian Girls on Plane Tell of Adoption Ordeal," *New York Times*, November 2, 1997, p. NE 39; "Russians Checking Up on Their Children Adopted by Americans," no author, *New York Times*, November 28, 1997, p. 24; Katharine Q. Seelye, "Judge Allows Couple to See Russian Girls," *New York Times*, December 24, 1997, p. 15.

11. Katharine Q. Seelye, "Judge Allows Couple to See Russian Girls," *New York Times*, December 24, 1997, p. 15.

12. Katharine Q. Seelye, "Adoptive Parents Win Battle for Russian Girls," *New York Times*, February 24, 1998, p. A10.

13. Katharine Q. Seelye, "Woman Sentenced to 22 Years in Death of Adopted Son," *New York Times*, September 23, 1997, p. 18.

14. *Diagnostic and Statistical Manual of Mental Disorders*, 4th ed. (Washington, D.C.: American Psychiatric Association, 1994), pp. 116–118.

15. "Russian Parliament Weighs Limiting Foreign Adoptions," *Baltimore Sun*, no author, November 29, 1997, p. 11; Alessandra Stanley, "U.S. Adoption Agencies Fear Tightening of Russian Laws," *New York Times*, December 4, 1997, p. 5.

16. International Resource Centre on the Protection of Children in Adoption, News Bulletin, no. 1 (June 1997), International Social Services, Geneva, Switzerland.

17. NCFA, "Russian Bill Would Deny Families for Thousands of Orphans," *National Adoption Reports*, vol. 18, no. 11 (November 1997): 5; op. cit., p. 49; op. cit., Seelye, November 2, 1997, p. 45. "Russians Checking Up on Their Chil-

dren Adopted by Americans," no author, *New York Times*, November 28, 1997, p. 24.

18. Op. cit., p. 16.

19. Sara Jay, "When Children Adopted Abroad Come with Too Many Troubles," *New York Times*, June 23, 1996, p. 1; Ellen Nakashima, "Untold Disabilities," *Washington Post*, June 18, 1996, p. 1; Reuter, "Overseas Adoption Problems," *Washington Post*, September 17, 1997, p. 2.

20. Elinor W. Ames, "Orphanage Experiences Play a Key Role in Adopted Romanian Children's Development," *"ADOPTALK"* (NACAC) (Fall 1997): 1; Katharine Q. Seelye, "Specialists Report Rise in Adoptions That Fail," *New York Times*, March 24, 1997, p. 14.

21. Seth Faison, "Chinese Happily Break the 'One Child' Rule," *New York Times*, August 17, 1997, p. A1; and Janny Scott, "Orphan Girls of China Find Eager US Parents," *New York Times*, August 19, 1997, p. A1.

22. Bob Herbert, "China's Missing Girls," *New York Times*, October 30, 1997, p. 39; Sheryl WuDunn, "Korean Women Still Feel Demands to Bear a Son," *New York Times*, January 14, 1997, p. 3.

23. Associated Press, "INS Probes Adoption Agencies Bringing Pregnant Russians to U.S.," *Washington Post*, April 16, 1998, p. 11.

24. Margaret Talbot, "Attachment Theory: The Ultimate Experiment," *New York Times Magazine*, May 24, 1998, p. 24.

25. Michael Riley, "Deceit Takes Babies Away in Honduras," *Baltimore Sun*, July 2, 1998, p. 2.

6

✛

A Comparison of the Experiences of Adult Korean and Black Transracial Adoptees

In this chapter we compare the experiences of the 124 white families who adopted 168 Korean children in the 1960s and 1970s against the experiences of the white families who participated in the Simon-Altstein twenty-year transracial adoption study (see chapter 4), in which two-thirds of the adoptees were black. The major foci are comparisons of the reactions that the adult Korean and black adoptees have to their Caucasian-American families, as well as comparisons of their racial/ethnic identities.

We report first the parents' reactions to their experiences: "Think back, and with the knowledge of hindsight and the experiences you have accumulated, would you have done again what you did—adopt a child of a different race?"

Ninety-five percent of the parents of the Korean adoptees and 92 percent of the parents of the mostly black transracial adoptees said "yes," that they would have done what they did—adopt a child of a different race. In each survey 3 and 4 percent were not sure and 2 percent said no. When asked "Why?" over 80 percent of the parents in both surveys who said they would do it again answered, "It was a positive, enriching, rewarding experience"; "because he/she is our child and we love him/her"; "he/she is like our birth child"; and "every child needs a home." Among the five families who said "no" or that they "weren't sure," two sets of parents said they adopted their children at nine and seven years of age, and the children had had traumatic experiences prior to being placed with them; five others cited pre-existing physical and emotional problems; and one family said, "Because we think our child would have been better off with a family of his own ethnic background."

We then asked: "With all the thought and preparation that went into your decision, what about the experience surprised you the most?"

The most frequent responses offered by over half of the respondents were: "There have been no major surprises"; "How easily our family and friends accepted our black (or Korean) son/daughter"; "How easy it was"; and "How quickly our child integrated/bonded with our family." Sixteen percent of the families in the longitudinal study commented on the paucity of information they had been given about their child's physical, emotional, and social backgrounds and how complicated the teen years were, "particularly how their child grappled with his/her identity." Five percent of the parents in the "Korean study" also commented about the difficulty surrounding identity issues during adolescence.

Almost all of the parents said that the main impact that rearing a child of a different racial and cultural background had on their lives was that "it exposed us to a different culture," "to different groups of people that we either would not have known or would not have known as well as we do"; "it broadened and enriched our lives"; "it made us more sensitive to racial issues, to what it means to be a minority"; "it made us more tolerant of all different kinds of people, from all walks of life"; and "we saw that an adopted child is no different than a biological child."

Finally, we asked the parents, "Would you recommend that other families like your own adopt a child of a different race or culture?"

Eighty percent of the parents in the longitudinal study and 90 percent in the Korean survey answered "yes," they would recommend that other families like their own adopt a child of a different race. Seventeen percent in the longitudinal survey and 10 percent in the Korean survey were not sure whether they would recommend transracial adoptions to other families similar to their own. Those who would recommend it said they would tell the family to "love the child as if it had been born to you," to "be aware that the child comes from a different culture" and try to expose him or her to that culture, and to be generally aware of the responsibility they are taking on. "The real issue is adoption, not transracial adoption." Others said, "It has to do with how you feel about raising a child who is not biologically your own. If you see it as second rate or second best, it will not work. Race is secondary to your general attitude about adoption"; and "It would need to be something that a family would embrace as a real encounter, a real mission, a family choice, a family direction in which to go. Never do it out of no other alternative to increasing the size of your family." The bottom line, for the large majority of the parents, is that adopting a child of a different race is a good thing to do.

What of the children, how did they respond to their adoptions?

At the time we conducted the last phase of the twenty-year study, the median age of the black adoptees was twenty-two; and 85 percent of them were no longer living at home. For the Korean adoptees, their median age in 1993 was twenty-eight, and 85 percent of them were also no longer living at home.

Twenty-four percent of the black adoptees and 30 percent of the Korean adoptees had completed at least a bachelor's degree. For over 60 percent of both the black and Korean TRAs, their parents had paid, or were paying, for all or part of their post-high school education.

Given the age difference between the Korean and black TRAs, it is not surprising that one-third of the former, compared to 13 percent of the latter, were married at the time of the interviews. None of the Koreans were married to a person of Korean birth, as compared to 20 percent of the black TRAs who had a black spouse.

A comparison of the types of work the respondents in each group reported they were engaged in is shown in table 6.1.

The higher percentage of Koreans who hold "professional" positions is probably a function of age, which in turn reflects years of schooling completed.

We had asked both groups of adoptees about the racial and ethnic

Table 6.1   Occupational Category in Percent

	Korean	*Black*
Professional	25	18
Administrative/Clerical	20	27
Skilled/Service	27	43
Other	11	3
Not Employed	17	16

characteristics of their three closest friends when they were adolescents and today (e.g., at the time of the interviews). The results are shown in table 6.2.

Especially as adults, the black TRAs are more likely to have "same race" friends than are the Koreans (we included anyone of Asian background). But for both groups the majority of their friends, during adolescence and as adults, were white.

When asked, "When you were dating in high school, were most of the people you dated white, black, Korean, Asian, or all different types?," 10 percent of the Korean and 47 percent of the black TRAs reported that they were not yet "into dating" when they were in high school. Among those who did date, 80 percent of the Koreans and 60 percent of the blacks dated whites almost exclusively. Thirty-eight percent of the blacks dated whites and blacks or blacks only (11 percent), compared to 5 percent of the Koreans who dated Asians. We have to remember that some of the bases for these responses are "who's out there," and with Asians representing 3.5 percent of the population, the opportunities for friendships and dates are more limited than they are for American blacks.

For the questions that focused on what it meant to the respondents to grow up in a family with a different racial background than their own, we found that 60 percent of the Koreans and 75 percent of the blacks did not remember when they first noticed the difference. Among those who had been adopted when they were four years or older, almost all said, "immediately" or "at the time I was adopted." Seventy-seven percent of the Koreans and almost 90 percent of the blacks said it made "little" or "no difference." Among those Koreans and blacks who felt it made a difference, their responses were divided

Table 6.2   Racial and Ethic Characteristics of Closest Friends

Friends	Percent Black TRAs		Percent Korean TRAs	
	High School	Current	High School	Current
		Friend #1		
White	73.2	53.0	87.8	79.7
Black	14.6	34.0	2.7	5.4
Asian	—	—	4.1	7.4
Latino	6.7	9.4	2.0	4.1
Other/Mixed	5.5	2.6	1.3	0.7
No Answer	5.5	2.6	1.3	0.7
		Friend #2		
White	70.8	70.0	87.2	87.2
Black	19.1	23.4	2.7	1.3
Asian	—	—	3.4	6.8
Latino	—	—	1.3	3.4
Other/Mixed	4.5	2.2	2.0	1.3
No Answer	5.6	4.4	3.4	0.0
		Friend #3		
White	61.8	70.0	84.5	81.8
Black	25.8	22.4	2.0	2.0
Asian	—	—	6.1	8.1
Latino	—	—	2.0	2.7
Other/Mixed	3.4	2.5	2.0	4.1
No Answer	9.0	5.1	3.4	1.3

almost equally into positive and negative effects. Their responses to the following item were also very similar:

> Was being of a different race and ethnicity than your adoptive family easier or harder during various stages of your life?

Forty-five percent of the Koreans and 40 percent of the blacks said they "never" or "rarely" thought about it. For the others, adolescence was the most difficult period, followed by early childhood.

In response to the item that asked how people of the same racial background as their own responded to them when they were adolescents, over half (53 percent) of the Koreans said there were very few or none around to make a difference. Among the Koreans who could answer substantively, 34 percent said, "It didn't seem to matter either positively or negatively." Thirty-seven percent of the blacks also made that response. Twenty-nine and 26 percent of the blacks and Koreans said they "reacted negatively toward me," and the other 30-plus percent said they received positive feedback.

In their responses to the following items about the quality of their relationships with each of their parents and their siblings during adolescence and currently, we see in table 6.3 that the large majority of both the Korean and black TRAs believe they had and continue to have close ties. Their ties are closer to the parents, especially their mothers, than they are with their siblings. There also appears to have been less change among the Korean TRAs between adolescence and young adulthood than there was among the black TRAs between adolescence and adulthood.

The item about the respondents' relationships with their siblings

Table 6.3   Quality of Relationship with Parents

Quality of Relationship with Mother	Koreans		Blacks	
	% Adolescent	% Adults	% Adolescent	% Adults
Very close	41.2	49.3	29.1	45.5
Fairly close	31.8	36.5	32.7	43.6
Quite distant	13.5	5.4	14.5	1.8
Distant	12.2	6.8	23.6	5.5
No Answer/Other	1.3	2.0	—	3.6

Quality of Relationship with Father	Koreans		Blacks	
	% Adolescent	% Adults	% Adolescent	% Adults
Very close	38.5	41.2	30.9	43.6
Fairly close	38.5	35.8	34.5	38.2
Quite distant	4.1	2.7	14.5	3.6
Distant	16.2	10.8	18.2	10.9
No Answer/Other*	2.7	9.4	1.8	3.6

*Deceased

was phrased somewhat differently on the Korean and black surveys, so that for the black TRAs we cannot identify whether the sibling is male or female, younger or older. Nevertheless, the results are worth comparing. Table 6.4 describes the Korean adoptees' responses.

Another way of assessing the quality of the TRAs' relationships to their families may be found in their responses to a series of questions that asked: "Who are the three people you would most likely turn to if you had a serious personal problem/money problem/were in trouble with the law?"

"Parents" were the people both the Korean and the black TRAs named most frequently for all three types of problems. They were followed by friends and then by siblings for both groups of respondents. The questions on the Korean survey were phrased "Who are the three people you would most likely turn to for help or advice?" The responses showed that 99, 95, and 93 percent of the Korean adoptees included their parents as one of the three people they would turn to

Table 6.4   Quality of Relationship with Siblings in Percent

| | Korean TRAs | | | | | | | |
| | Very Close | | Fairly Close | | Quite Distant | | Distant | |
Sibling	Adolescent	Adult	Adolescent	Adult	Adolescent	Adult	Adolescent	Adult
Older Brother(s)	30	30	37	40	18	15	15	15
Older Sister(s)	29	29	43	46	12	13	16	12
Younger Brother(s)	33	30	50	46	7	8	10	16
Younger Sister(s)	27	24	47	48	11	8	15	14
	Black TRAs							
	Very Close		Fairly Close		Quite Distant		Distant	
	Adolescent	Adult	Adolescent	Adult	Adolescent	Adult	Adolescent	Adult
Sibling #1	27.3	30.9	30.9	43.6	18.2	10.9	20.0	12.7
Sibling #2	25.0	20.9	45.4	48.8	15.9	9.3	13.6	20.9

for personal, money, or legal problems. Friends were cited second by 73, 42, and 53 percent of the respondents for each of the problems, and siblings third (48, 34, and 40 percent).

On the longitudinal survey we asked: "Who are the first, second, and third persons you would seek out if you had a serious personal problem/money problem/were in trouble with the law?" Parents were the first persons named for all three problems, followed by friends and siblings.

Contrary to reports in the media and popular literature, few of either the Korean or black TRAs tried to locate their birth parents: 8 percent for the Koreans and 25 percent for the blacks. Among the blacks, all but one only tried to locate their birth mothers; for the Koreans, the few who did try, sought to locate both parents. Almost all of the adopted parents helped the black TRAs and half of them were successful in locating the birth mothers. Among the eleven Koreans, all of them turned to the Holt Agency for help, and one did locate her birth mother. With such small numbers, there doesn't appear to be much point in pursuing the issue.

On a policy issue, when asked, "Would you urge social workers and adoption agencies to place Hispanic, Korean, Asian, black and other nonwhite children in white homes?" 86 percent of the Koreans and 70 percent of the black TRAs said "yes." The blacks who said "yes" did so without any stipulations, whereas most of the Koreans had some stipulations, though many of them were unrelated to race. The 30 percent of the blacks who had stipulations focused on the importance of finding white families "who are willing to make a commitment to exposing the child to his or her birth culture."

Toward the end of the interview, the respondents were asked to describe themselves (see table 6.5). Almost a third of the black and Korean TRAs identified themselves as such. Describing themselves as mixed is probably an accurate description for many of the respondents in both groups. But the 20 percent among the Korean respondents who describe themselves as "white" are dissembling. Remember, Kim reported that 25 percent of the Korean adoptees in his study believed that they belonged to the American groups; 8 percent identified with the Korean groups and the rest identified with the Korean-

Table 6.5   Respondents' Description of Self

Korean	Percent	Black	Percent
Korean	30	Black	32
Asian	5	Mixed: Black/White	68
Mixed: Korean/Asian/American	32		
White	20		
American	7		
Other	6		

American group; even though more than 60 percent of the subjects were racially pure Korean.

The question was followed by: "How do you think being (Korean/ black) by birth but reared by white parents has affected how you perceive yourself today?"

One-third of the Korean and one-third of the black TRAs said in essence, "It did not affect my self-image one way or the other." One-third of the blacks and one-third of the Koreans thought it had a positive effect. One-third of the blacks said they did not know what effect it had—none said it had a negative impact. Among the Koreans, some 20 percent thought it had a negative effect, with 5 percent stating explicitly, "It made me feel like a banana."

As for the advice they would give to white parents who have the opportunity to adopt a young child of their (the respondents') racial background, over 91 percent of the black TRAs said, in essence, "Do it, but be sensitive to racial issues." The Korean responses were somewhat more diverse; 10 percent, for example, said, "Just do it," but at least 60 percent mentioned being sensitive to the child's birth culture as important advice they would give.

CONCLUDING REMARKS

In sum, the findings reported in this chapter show remarkable similarities in the experiences of both the parents and the Korean and black TRAs. In their perception of themselves, in their life experiences, in their relationships with their parents and siblings, in the advice they would offer to families considering a transracial adoption, and in their support for the practice as a policy matter and for the positive personal results it produced, on all of these issues Korean and black TRAs are in agreement. And for almost all of the parents of these children, the experience was joyous, positive, and enriching.

7

+

The Experiences of Stars of David Families: 1987 and 1997

This chapter describes and compares the experiences of an adoptive-parent network called the Stars of David (SOD), composed of people who have adopted children across both racial and national lines. The first survey of "Stars of David" families was conducted in 1987 and involved 59 parents who had adopted 94 children in the Boston, New York City, and Washington, D.C., communities. The interviews were conducted in the respondents' homes. The second survey was conducted by mail ten years later in 1997 and included 204 sets of parents from all parts of the United States, who had adopted 302 children.

The Stars of David is a Boston-based nationwide adoptive parent group comprised of Jewish (or intermarried) couples whose avowed purpose is to rear the children they adopt as Americans, as Jews, and with a knowledge and respect for the culture of their birth. Thus, a Korean boy adopted into a Stars of David family is likely to receive a "Hebrew" name, undergo circumcision, and have a Bar Mitzvah. A Colombian girl will also participate in a naming ceremony and may have a Bat Mitzvah. Both will learn about their birth culture through language, books, food, travel, and observance of ceremonies and rituals. Both will be American children, legally and socially, as a function of their adoption, their environment, and their lifestyles. Since its founding in the early 1980s, the Stars of David has grown from 35 families in Boston and its suburbs to over 700 families who are spread across the country.

The racial and ethnic characteristics of the children in the two surveys are shown in table 7.1.

In both surveys, over 80 percent of the families adopted their first child when he or she was less than one year old. Fifty-six percent of the parents in the first survey and 76 percent of the families in the second survey chose to adopt because they were infertile.

The demographic characteristics of the parents in the two surveys were very similar. They ranged in age from 30 to 60; most were between 40 and 45 years old. Over 75 percent had master's degrees and Ph.D.s or professional degrees in law, business, engineering, and medicine. The husbands worked mainly as lawyers, engineers, doctors, business executives, professors, and computer experts. In both surveys one-third of the wives were full-time homemakers; the others worked mostly as teachers, as social workers, or in business.

JEWISH PRACTICES AND TIES TO THE COMMUNITY

In the first survey, 35 percent of the families were members of a synagogue before they adopted their first child; in the second survey, half

Table 7.1   Racial and Ethnic Characteristics of Adopted Children

	1987 Survey	*1997 Survey*
Korean	36	42
Hispanic	22	96
Other Asian	9	24*
Russian/Eastern Europe	—	22
American Black	9	19
Native American	2	—
American White	16	99
Total	94	302

*India, 11; China, 13

of the families were members. In both surveys most of the families (over two-thirds) discussed their plans to adopt a child of a different race or nationality with their rabbis, and, with one or two exceptions, received a positive and supportive response. In both surveys, 80 percent of the families had their adopted children undergo a formal conversion ceremony and almost all plan to have them be a Bar or Bat Mitzvah when the boys are thirteen and the girls are twelve years old. While the parents were highly educated in the secular realm, three-quarters of them reported that they received little in the way of a formal Jewish education as they were growing up. In the first survey, only three of the mothers and two of the fathers attended a Jewish day school. In the second survey, 13 percent of the mothers and 16 percent of the fathers reported going to a Jewish day school. About half of the mothers and fathers in both surveys attended a Hebrew school a few times a week after they finished their public school day.

Only a small fraction of the families (less than 10 percent) in both surveys attend synagogue on a daily or even weekly basis, most attend a Reform or Conservative synagogue only on the "High Holidays" (New Year's and the Day of Atonement). In table 7.2, a large majority of the families report observing rituals on a regular basis.

When asked to indicate which, if any, of the observances in table 7.3 they thought were "very important," "somewhat important," or "not important" for their children to follow, a large majority listed several of them as very important.

Having Jewish friends was of little importance to almost all of the respondents in both surveys. On the other matters, where there were differences in the two surveys, they were all in the direction of more

Table 7.2   Percent Who Observed Rituals in Adoptive Families

Observe Ritual	First Survey	Second Survey
Light Sabbath candles	59	58
Have a Mezuzah on the door	95	94
Attend High Holiday services	91	93
Fast on Yom Kippur	80	81
Perform or attend a Seder	95	96
Light Chanukah candles	97	98

Table 7.3   Percentage of Importance of Observances

Observance	First Survey	Second Survey
Be educated about Jewish history/culture	88	90
Marry a Jew	26	53
Observe Jewish holidays	57	78
Contribute to Jewish charities	43	58
Participate in Jewish community life	34	67
Have mostly Jewish friends	4	15
Observe Jewish rituals and customs	41	61
Take pride in being a Jew	93	94

respondents placing importance on the observances in the 1997 survey. Note especially the differences in the importance of marrying someone who is Jewish, participating in Jewish community life, and observing Jewish rituals. Over two-thirds of the families belong to at least one Jewish organization in addition to the Stars of David. Hadassah was the one most frequently mentioned in both surveys.

Retaining ties to their adopted child's culture was important to most of the parents, as witnessed by the fact that over 70 percent in both surveys (71 percent in 1997 and 75 percent in 1987) reported that they had spent time learning about their adopted child's birth culture and as a family engaged in ceremonies and rituals that are derived from that culture. The "ethnic" experiences that the families described include preparing special foods, having cultural artifacts and books in their homes, attending classes about their child's birth culture, belonging to ethnic organizations, establishing ties with families who have children of that culture, and learning the language of their child's birth culture. Indeed, only a handful of the families said that they did not engage in any of the previous activities because they felt that it was the Jewish identity, culture, and heritage that the children should live with and inherit.

To find out how the parents perceived their relationship with their children (adopted and birth), we devised a four-point scale that asked the parents to indicate whether they evaluated the relationship as (1) positive and good; (2) positive aspects outweigh negative aspects; (3)

negative aspects outweigh positive; and (4) negative and bad. If the parent checked any category save "(1) positive and good," we asked that they explain the problems they were having with a given child. In the 1987 survey, 83 percent of the parents checked "1" (positive and good). Only one family said that the negative aspects of their relationship outweighed the positive ones in dealing with any of their birth children. An additional three said that there were some problems, but, all things considered, "the positive factors outweighed the negative ones." Those families described the problems as "emotional" and "personality." The parents in one family who checked "negative outweighs positive" described drugs, drinking, and anger directed at them.

The picture was somewhat more complicated for the adopted children. For their first adoptee, 68 percent of the families checked "1" positive and good, ten families checked "2," there are problems but the positive outweighs the negative; six of the parents checked "3," negative outweighs positive; and nine checked "4," negative and bad, in describing their relationships with their first adopted child. None of the twenty-three families who adopted more than one child checked "3" or "4." Six said that there were problems, but the positive factors outweighed the negative. The problems most frequently described were disobedience, anger, and emotional and personality problems. Three families mentioned drugs and drinking.

In the 1997 survey the picture was somewhat different. For their first adoptee 82 percent of the families checked (1) positive and good; 15 percent checked (2) there are problems but the positive elements outweigh the negative ones; 2 percent checked (3) the problems are such that the negative elements outweigh the positive ones; and 1 percent checked (4) negative and bad. The ratings for the second adopted child were even more positive: 88 percent were rated (1), 11 percent were rated (2), and one percent were rated (3). For the few families who adopted more than two children, the ratings were much the same. In the 1997 survey the parents rated their relationships with their birth children less positively for the first birth child, 69 percent of the ratings were a (1), 28 percent were a (2), and 4 percent were a (3). For the second birth child the ratings were 74 percent (1), 23 percent (2), and 3 percent (3). Just as families rarely had more than two adopted children, too few families had more than two birth children (15) for the ratings to be reported in detail, except to say that they were much like those reported for the families having one and two birth children.

Thus, comparing the responses in the earlier and later surveys, we found that in 1987, 83 percent of the parents checked "1," positive and good, in characterizing their relationships with their 34 birth children, and 68 percent of the parents checked "1" in characterizing their relationship with all of their 94 adopted children. Among parents who adopted two children, 58 percent rated the relationship with their first adoptee a "1" and 74 percent rated their relationship with their second adoptee a "1." There are not enough birth children to make comparable examinations.

In 1997, 69 percent of the parents checked "1" in characterizing their relationship with their 98 birth children, and 83 percent of the parents checked "1" in characterizing their relationship with their 253 adopted children. In the second survey the ratings for the first and second adopted child were very similar, 82 and 88 percent. Overall, the parents rated their relationships with their adopted children more positively than they did their relationships with their birth children.

When we asked the parents what advice they have to offer families like themselves who are considering adoption, in the 1987 survey, 62 percent urged it unequivocally and 25 percent urged the family to adopt but only after they had thought about it long and hard and were sure of their own motivations. Nine percent would say only that the family should think long and hard before they did anything, and 4 percent, which consisted of two families, advocated against adoption. In the 1997 survey, even though the relationship ratings were more positive, 53 percent recommended it unequivocally, for example, "Go for it," "Don't hesitate." Others said they would advise the families to adopt but would tell them to "be certain they can handle the pressures that arise from obvious differences," "be sure they understand the child's needs," "are willing to provide the child with a sense of his or her culture," and "be prepared to become a transcultural and/or a transracial family, not parents who have adopted a child's country or a different race."

Only in the 1987 survey were we able to interview the birth and adopted children who were at least six years of age. The following section describes what the children had to say about their experiences. In total, we interviewed 60 children, 23 birth and 37 adopted. The racial and ethnic backgrounds of the adopted children who were old enough to be interviewed are as follows: Korean 13, other Asian 3, Hispanic 11, American black 9, American white 1.

DEMOGRAPHIC AND EDUCATIONAL CHARACTERISTICS OF THE ADOPTED AND BIRTH CHILDREN

The birth children ranged in age from 6 to 23 and the adoptees from 6 to 21. The median age for the birth interviewees was 11.4 and for the adoptees 9.8 years. For the birth children, their years in school ranged from second grade to college, and for the adoptees, from kindergarten to college. The median school year for the birth children was eighth grade and for the adoptees fourth grade. Forty-five percent of both the birth and adopted children were boys. Three out of five of the birth interviewees were the oldest child in the family and one out of three of the adoptees was the oldest.

Fourteen percent of the birth children and 22 percent of the adoptees were attending Jewish day schools. Three out of five of the birth children who were in the appropriate age categories were attending Hebrew classes after school, compared to two out of five of the adoptees; but more of the adoptees were attending Jewish day schools. Altogether, fourteen of the twenty-one birth children in the appropriate age range were attending either Jewish day schools or Hebrew classes after school, compared to fifteen out of the twenty-nine adoptees in the appropriate age range. For both the birth and adopted children, the percentages are high compared to a cross section of the American Jewish community in those cities. Forty-three percent of the adoptees speak, read, and/or write Hebrew, in contrast to 30 percent of the birth children. Only two of the adopted children speak, read, and write Spanish; an additional two speak but do not read or write Spanish. Four birth children also speak Spanish. None report that they speak, read, or write Korean. From these responses, it seems clear that the adoptees are not retaining or learning the language of their birth cultures.

OBSERVANCE OF JEWISH PRACTICES

A comparison of the responses of the birth and adopted children to the items in table 7.4, describing the Jewish ritual and ceremonial observances that the families engage in on a regular basis, reveals little difference between the two groups. The large majority report observance of the major holidays, but they do not observe the regular daily or weekly activities such as dietary laws and the Sabbath.

Like their parents, only a small group, two of the birth children and six of the adoptees, report that they and their families attend temple or synagogue on a regular basis. Eighty-seven percent of the children born into the families and 80 percent of the adoptees report having had, or planning to have, a Bar or Bat Mitzvah. Over the past year, 42 percent of the birth and 27 percent of the adopted children reported having read at least one book about Jewish history or culture. Three of the adopted children reported reading a book about their birth culture.

Looking ahead, we asked the children about whether they expected to participate in Jewish community life when they were adults and on

Table 7.4   Percent of Families Who Observe Jewish Rituals and Ceremonies

	Regulary Engaged	
Observance	*Birth*	*Adopted*
Observe dietary laws	21.7	17.7
Light Sabbath candles	39.1	38.2
Attend synagogue on Rosh Hashanah	91.3	90.6
Fast part or all of Yom Kippur	70.0	62.0
Light candles on Chanukah	95.6	97.2
Attend a Seder on Passover	91.3	94.1
Dress up for Purim	56.5	59.4
Help build or sit in a Sukka	69.6	79.6

their own. Sixty-four percent of the birth and 57 percent of the adopted children said they did, mostly by joining a temple or synagogue.

IDENTITY AND SELF-ESTEEM

When the adopted children were asked whether it bothered them that they looked different from their parents, two-thirds said it was not a source of difficulty and it caused them no problems. Three of the ten children who mentioned specific problems said that they were uncomfortable at extended family functions on Jewish occasions. Twenty-two of the adopted children also recalled problems that they had within the past three years with children calling them names and making fun of them because of their racial backgrounds. Two-thirds ignored the incident, but later, half either told their parents about it or reported what had happened to a teacher.

In response to the question that asked each child to explain how he or she would describe himself or herself to a stranger, none of the birth children mentioned physical characteristics or religion; they all described personality characteristics. In contrast, 37 percent of the adopted children mentioned race, religion, and the fact that they were adopted. The same distribution, approximately one-third, mentioned racial, religious, and adoptive status characteristics as opposed to personality traits among the intercountry adoptees and the other adoptees.

The Self-Esteem Scale developed by Morris Rosenberg and Roberta Simmons in 1968 remains one of the most frequently used and reliable measures of this concept to date. It has been used in countless studies, including the longitudinal survey that we began in 1972. We used the Self-Esteem Scale again in this study and report the results in table 7.5.

On five of the nine items, the birth children were more likely to take a positive attitude about themselves, to believe they have a number of good qualities, and to feel well satisfied with themselves. But the adopted children were less likely to feel that they are "no good," "a failure," or that they do not have much about which to feel proud. It is interesting that the adopted children scored higher when they re-

Table 7.5 Percent High Self-Esteem* Scores by Children's Status

Items	Adopted	Birth
1. I take a positive attitude toward myself (Strongly Agree)	32.1	47.6
2. I wish I could have more respect for myself (Strongly Disagree)	16.7	15.0
3. I certainly feel useless at times (Strongly Disagree)	4.2	15.8
4. I feel I have a number of good qualities (Strongly Agree)	37.0	52.4
5. All in all, I am inclined to feel that I am a failure (Strongly Disagree)	64.3	50.0
6. I am able to do things as well as most other people (Strongly Agree)	21.4	33.3
7. I feel I do not have much to be proud of (Strongly Disagree)	48.0	31.1
8. On the whole, I am well satisfied with myself (Strongly Agree)	28.0	55.0
9. At times I think I am no good (Strongly Disagree)	20.0	9.5

*As measured by a "Strongly Agree" or "Strongly Disagree" response depending on which is appropriate for determining High Self-Esteem.

sponded against a negative image, in contrast to the birth children who made more direct positive assessments of themselves. In other words, the adopted children are more likely to assert their self-esteem in response to negative assessments such as "I feel I do not have much to be proud of" or "I think I'm no good."

FAMILY TIES AND INTEGRATION

There were no differences in the relationships that the birth and adopted children had with their grandparents, aunts and uncles, and other relatives. For almost all the children, the ties were positive. For a few, the relatives lived far away and visits were infrequent.

In a series of items that asked, "Who knows best who you are," "to whom would you be most likely to go if you were happy about something," "if you were worried about something," and "if you were accused of stealing," we found no significant differences in the preferences expressed by birth and adopted children (see table 7.6).

Parents and siblings, as opposed to nonfamily members, were the most likely targets for both the birth and adopted children.

Another measure of the extent to which the adopted and birth children believed themselves to be an integral part of their families may be observed by comparing scores on the "family integration scale," which was used on the British Adoption Project (BAP). The birth and adopted children were asked to respond to the items in table 4.7.

On three of the eight items the adopted and birth children responded differently. On the "trust" and "stick by me" items, the birth children indicated more of a sense of family integration than did the adopted children. On the "treated in the same way" item, the adopted children demonstrated a greater sense of family integration.

When we probed further about the quality of their relationships with their parents and asked about the ties they expected to have to them in the future, 74 percent of the birth children, compared to 43 percent of the adopted children, said "very close." The remaining 26 percent of the birth children answered "close," while 50 percent of the adopted children said "close" and 7 percent said "fairly close." These responses are not inconsistent with the parents' responses in the 1987 survey. When the parents were asked about their relationships with

Table 7.6 Respondents' Perceptions of Family versus Nonfamily* as an Integral Part of Identity

	Birth		Adopted	
	Parent & Siblings	Nonfamily	Parent & Siblings	Nonfamily
Who knows best who you are	52.2	47.8	57.6	42.4
Happy about something	64.2	35.8	64.5	35.5
Worried about something	57.1	42.9	68.2	31.8
Wrongly accused of stealing	66.6	33.4	63.0	37.0

*Includes friends, teachers, police, store owner

Table 7.7   Family Integrative Scale by Children's Status

Family Integration Items	Birth	Adopted
I enjoy family life		
Strongly agree	54.6	45.2
Agree	45.4	51.6
Disagree	—	—
Strongly disagree	—	—
I would like to leave home as soon as possible when I am able to*		
Strongly agree	—	7.7
Agree	33.3	30.8
Disagree	50.0	46.2
Strongly disagree	16.7	15.4
People in our family trust one another		
Strongly agree	45.5	23.3
Agree	54.5	60.0
Disagree	—	10.0
Strongly disagree	—	6.7
Most families are happier than ours		
Strongly disagree	27.8	29.6
Disagree	72.2	63.0
Agree	—	7.4
Strongly agree	—	—
I am treated in the same way as my brothers and sisters		
Strongly agree	18.2	21.4
Agree	40.9	53.6
Disagree	31.8	17.9
Strongly disagree	9.1	7.1
Most children are closer to their parents than I am		
Strongly disagree	42.9	25.0
Disagree	42.9	66.7
Agree	14.3	8.3
Strongly agree	—	—
If I am in trouble, I know my parents will stick by me		
Strongly agree	52.4	31.0
Agree	47.6	55.2
Disagree	—	10.3
Strongly disagree	—	3.5
My parents know what I am really like as a person		
Strongly agree	42.9	27.6
Agree	47.6	65.5
Disagree	9.5	6.9
Strongly disagree	—	—

*The Ns on this item are smaller: 12 for the birth children and 13 for the adopted. We keep the item because the distributions are similar to the others in which the Ns range from 18 to 31.

their adopted children, 68 percent rated them as positive and good, compared to 83 percent of the parents who rated their relationships with their birth children as positive and good. We also asked about the ties the birth and adopted children expected to have to each other, but, unfortunately, the numbers were too small to make the responses worth comparing.

CONCLUDING REMARKS

The Stars of David parents, like most adoptive parents, are clearly middle class, are educated, and work as professionals. They live in predominantly white neighborhoods. Over 75 percent opted to adopt because they could not bear children or because they could not bear any more after they had their first child. Two-thirds of the families did not have any birth children. The parents waited an average of 6.5 years from the time of their marriage until they adopted their first child. In the first survey, most of the children came from Korea; in the second, the majority come from Latin America; and in both surveys they were less than one year of age at the time of adoption.

Across the two surveys, between 35 and 50 percent of the SOD families reported belonging to a synagogue, but less than 10 percent said they attended synagogue or temple on a weekly basis. Over 70 percent of both groups of families reported engaging in ceremonies and rituals derived from their adopted children's birth culture, having books and artifacts in their homes about their children's culture, seeking out Korean and Hispanic friends, and joining "ethnic organizations."

We conclude with a few observations about the implications for social work practice. Along with normal developmental struggles, foreign-born intercountry adoptees who are being raised as American Jews have to come to terms with being loyal to their birth culture and racial identity while maintaining integrity with their adopted religion and its traditions. Social workers should be alert to the difficulties inherent in this struggle.

In additional, social workers treating potential adoptive parents, or families who have already adopted foreign-born children, and/or the intercountry adoptees themselves, must be aware of the complex set of issues involved in this type of adoption. Particularly during adolescence when, at best, many adoptees are confused and conflicted about "who they are," social workers should be sensitive to the possibility that intercountry adoptees may demonstrate additional confusion. The social worker should help prepare the adoptive parents for the struggles that are likely to occur with this type of adoption.

The possibility of negative reactions toward these children by the Jewish community, particularly when dating begins, is another issue with which social workers may have to deal.

Finally, what seems to be universally agreed upon is the importance of linkage with an adoptive-parent support group such as the Stars of David. This connection appears critical for all concerned. We recommend that social workers actively encourage adoptive families to join local branches of this organization. It provides the comfort of a common identity, along with the realization that there are other families living through similar situations. More important, it offers an opportunity for sharing successful problem-solving techniques associated with commonly experienced circumstances.

8

✢

Concluding Remarks and Policy Recommendations

A message that comes through loudly and clearly from all of the empirical studies that have been cited in this book is that transracial and intercountry adoptions serve the children's best interests. And children are and should be the main concern of adoption policies and practices. Whether the study focuses on African-American children adopted by white parents; Korean children adopted by American parents; or Hispanic, Asian, Eastern European, and African-American children adopted by Jewish American families, the results show that the children feel loved, secure, committed to their adopted families, and comfortable with their racial/ethnic identities. For those studies that reported findings among adult adoptees, the results were comparable. The adoptions served the adoptees' best interests. They felt they had been loved and wanted by their adoptive families, and they were secure in their ethnic and racial identities.

Another, and probably equally important, message that comes through from these studies is that "love is not enough." In order to rear emotionally healthy, stable, and secure children, the families had to adjust and expand their lifestyles to include learning about and making contact with their adoptive children's cultural and racial/ethnic history and heritage. As important as it was for parents to treat

141

adopted children and love them as if they were birth children, it was not enough and could even be detrimental. As we saw in some of the comments made by the adult African-American adoptees, treating them as if they were birth children sometimes meant that their parents failed to provide them with the experiences they needed to understand their black American culture and history. As reported in some of the studies, not all of the parents recognized how much they needed to alter their lifestyles until several years after the adoption and sometimes not until the adoptees were adolescents.

Prior to recent federal legislation (the Multi-Ethnic Placement Act in 1994 and the Adoption and Safe Families Act in 1997), transracial adoptions were governed by the same laws as other adoptions; they were the province of the states. The laws of the state in which the adoption is to take place control the arrangements. The main purpose of the federal acts was to prohibit the use of race to delay or deny the placement of a child for adoption or foster care. Some states, prior to the passage of the Adoption and Safe Families Act, still made race a significant factor in adoption decisions. At the time this book went to press, there were no reliable data about the effectiveness of the statute in enhancing the opportunities for transracial adoptions.

Intercountry adoptions require that the adoption comply with the law of the child's birth country, U.S. immigration law, and the laws of the state in which the adoptive parents live. On October 1, 1994, the INS implemented a law that requires both birth parents to approve their child's adoption into the United States. As described in chapter 2, the law was passed primarily to prevent challenges to the adoption by putative fathers who might claim, months or even years after the adoption, that they were not consulted and do not approve of the adoption.

According to State Department statistics, in 1998 American families adopted 15,774 children from overseas, with Russia and China accounting for more than half of that number. Reliable U.S. data are not available on the number of transracial adoptions within the United States, but based on adoption agencies' reports they are probably about half that number. Given that estimates indicate that some 85,000 U.S. children are available for adoption and about half of those are African-American children, and that all of the research data indicate that transracial adoptions serve the child's best interests, the message is clear. We should make it easier for minority children to be moved out of institutions or foster care and should place them in permanent, stable, loving families.

IMPLICATIONS FOR SOCIAL WORK PRACTICE

This book described the experiences of white American families who adopted children. That these children were native-born African American, Native American, foreign-born Asian, Hispanic, or white was not a controlling issue for most of these adoptive parents. They wanted to parent a child. They received a child. It was the world outside that at times made their decision controversial and made parents defensive of their decision to adopt.

Adoption is often not simple. Even when adopters are "matched" to (healthy) adoptees in terms of physical characteristics, including race, adoption is often complex.[1] When racial and ethnic differences between adopters and children are added, finding a permanent home for parentless children becomes entangled in culture, law, politics, economics, historical prejudices both perceived and real, and personal bias. To understand the history of transracial adoption in this country is to appreciate the politics of race on its most intimate level. We acknowledge that with good cause, resulting from a history of slavery followed by blatant forms of institutional racism, many African-American groups remain suspicious of transracial adoption and have strong feelings against it.

The development of TRA was not a result of deliberate agency programming but an accommodation to perceived reality. Social changes regarding abortion, contraception, single parenthood, and reproduction in general have reduced the number of white children available for adoption, leaving nonwhite children as the largest available source. Changes also occurred regarding the willingness of white couples to adopt nonwhite children.

Those opposed to transracial adoption challenged its two main assumptions: (1) that it is necessary to place black children with white families because there are insufficient black families available to adopt black children; and (2) that benefits derived by a black child in a transracial adoption surpass those received in any other inracial, albeit temporary, placement.

In 1999 TRA continues to be opposed on the previously cited grounds, although at times the debate has become more caustic. But arguments today against TRA are largely academic, for one simple reason . . . most agencies are no longer willing to support TRA as a permanency plan for nonwhite children, the recent federal statutes notwithstanding. It has been suggested that agencies might attempt to subvert the 1994 and 1997 statutes with the (mis)use of family preservation programs, with kinship care, and by supporting the reintroduction of the orphanage.[2]

Curiously, adding an international component, in which non-U.S.-born nonwhite children are adopted by white American families, does not make adoption more complex. In fact, in some ways the reverse may be true: It simplifies matters. Why? Because adopting a foreign-born child generally does not carry the historical "baggage" of the relationship between African Americans and whites in this country. True, there are other issues of wealth, power, race, deception, kidnapping, class exploitation, colonialism, and imperialism, but these conditions are not as "close to home" as the troubled and at times violent history of race in the United States.

Intercountry adoption involves private and public agencies and organizations, governments, churches, lawyers, judges, social workers, nongovernmental organizations (NGOs), administrators, and bureaucrats of all types. Most of these individuals and organizations are honest and professional. Some are not. Intercountry adoptions consist of families of all designs, from traditional relationships of married men and women with and without birth and/or adopted children; to women and men living together without marriage; single adults, both women and men; gay individuals and couples; and so forth.

The conviction that race is the overpowering predictor in a person's life dies hard. Despite all the positive experiences described by adult transracial adoptees of growing up in white families, which were reported in the professional literature of several disciples, despite very strongly worded federal legislation prohibiting the use of race in adoption and foster care, "*. . . even as one of a group of reasons routinely* *used when making placement decisions,"* organizations continue to support the use of race as vital to a child's best interests.[3] Political correctness, it seems, keeps some organizations behind the curve of empirical evidence, social attitudes, and federal statutes.

Intercountry adoption does have one defining characteristic common to all types of adoption: the issue of social class. The rich (white) adopting the children of the poor (nonwhite). It is as old a story as the biblical one involving the Pharaoh's daughter finding Moses in the bulrushes and rearing him as an Egyptian prince. Although the conditions leading to intercountry adoptions are different from other forms of adoption, all adoptions nonetheless share a common script not significantly changed over time. The issues separating ICA from other adoption designs are the issues of ethnicity, race, and the globalization of our world today, leading to the relative elimination of national borders. In microcosm, ICA may be the story of race relations on a global scale.

ICA also is connected to a country's social, economic, and political stability because in most cases there is a link between the weaknesses of these social institutions and the likelihood that any given country will see it as being in their self-interest to allow foreign nationals to adopt their children.

More important, ICA also involves the social value placed on gender. Operationally, this means that most intercountry adoptees are female. The latter, being less desirable and less valued in their birth country, are the ones most frequently sent abroad. In this case, a negative status in one's birth culture results in removal to a society where opportunities are likely to be greater and life is more secure.

What separates social work from other areas of social science is that social work emphasizes practice. Practice, be it with groups, organizations, individuals, or families, is what social workers do. Social work deals with people, hands on. Its roots lie in social activism, what is now called community organization, and it all started at about the turn of the twentieth century with the early settlement-house movement in cities such as New York and Chicago. Historically, social work has suffered the label of being "intuitive." It has been defined as a field dominated by female "do-gooders" whose hearts were in the right place but whose involvement in people's lives was value-driven, resting on self-defined virtuousness, not research findings. After many decades of struggle, social work practice is now largely data-based—at least, that's what schools of social work and social welfare agencies espouse in their curricula, accreditation documents, and organizational materials.

Given this, it is understandable that almost every piece of research in child welfare (one of social work's main practice areas) in the last few decades ends with a somewhat romantic section entitled "Policy and Practice Recommendations." It is at this time that investigators, ripe with wisdom from their just-concluded study, venture onto the high-wire of the future by suggesting ways and means by which their area of interest can be improved in the real world of practice. By and large, these chapters are exercises in wheel spinning. Why? In the case of adoption, when practice recommendations are put into operation the process often appears immune to the logic of research findings. It seems as if law, policy, practice, and data live in separate worlds, almost unaware of each others' existence.

Theory holds that statutes and research findings should influence policy, which in turn should drive practice. An example of how this could operate should have been witnessed in the passage of MEPA, the 1994 federal statute (see chapter 2). MEPA was passed with the strong support of many decades of empirical research to support transracial adoption. In a very real sense, data drove the design and implementation of this statute. Researchers, law professors, and other experts testified many times before local, state, and federal legislative committees, describing their data and in other ways bolstering cross-racial adoption. Transracial adoption works for the children. It works for the families. It works for society. There were no axes to be ground. Racially different independent investigators came to similar conclusions, based on their own empirical examinations. Public opinion of all races supported placing children with racially different families if a family of their own race was unavailable. Transracial adoption was in the best interests of the child, this criterion being one of the fundamental axioms of child welfare practice. Yet many agencies and social workers practice as if there were no data supporting this type of permanent placement for parentless children and as if there were no statutes forbidding the use of race in child placement. Why, then, complain for so long that social work is unscientific and subsequently discard empirical findings based on the scientific method? Why champion scientific practice and then define the resultant data as optional? If social workers and agencies only recognize data they agree with, let's return to intuition because that's what social workers and agencies are in fact doing by ignoring statute and data, relying on what they "think" will work.

Social work's attitude toward TRA paradoxically runs against its historic raison d'être. As a social movement, social work came into being by working with society's unwanted, the intergenerationally poor, historically disenfranchised, and immigrant groups. Social work helped create and operate the settlement houses, which served as way stations into America's mainstream. Social work was, at its birth, an "unconventional" profession that many times supported unpopular causes. Social workers took these positions because in their estimation they were morally correct. As time passed and social work became institutionalized among America's professions, it sought the ingredients of any profession, a foundation of indigenous theory upon which to base its own particular practice (e.g., intervention strategies).

In 1997 MEPA, in the form of the Adoption and Safe Families Act, was passed with teeth. If agencies receiving federal dollars did not comply with its mandates, real financial consequences would follow. Compliance is not voluntary. Behavior is not probabilistic. If the law says race should not be a factor when considering placing a child for adoption or in selecting an adoptive family, then that's the way it should be. Social workers are not given a choice as to whether they want to comply. It is the law. They must comply. Yet in practice compliance seems a rarity. Political agendas, it appears, still reign. It's as if the law was optional or simply not there.

The future of adoption policy and practice, as is the case with other areas, is often tied to political trends and considerations. Many times, scientifically derived data either supporting or challenging a particular policy or program are one of the least convincing forms of evidence one can muster. For the most part, political and social zeitgeists seem more powerful determinants of programs and practice interventions, and here we speak directly to TRA, its detractors, and those supporting their claims.

"Political correctness" has been very popular in the 1990s. It has a few variations, but essentially it is defined as behavior sensitive to the popular liberal positions of the times, regardless of its actual effect in society. Politically correct thinking was very much in evidence in most social workers' attitudes toward transracial adoption. As the twentieth century closes, the standard, almost rote-like, arguments made against TRA by those a priori opposed to it are that (1) there would be more than sufficient numbers of black families to adopt all available black children were it not for racist adoption practices that prevent them from doing so, and that (2) black children adopted by white parents develop into racially confused adults, no matter how hard their parents try to develop a sense of black pride in their adopted children and no matter what research says to the contrary.[4] According to the politically correct rhetoric, white parents cannot succeed in instilling a sense of history and racial self-respect in their black children.

CONCLUSION

After three decades and several volumes of research, this is our final examination of transracial adoption. The data we have accumulated over the decades deserve serious consideration. We entered this area of inquiry with no social or political agenda. We exit with none.

We were interested in looking at how the races could live together in so intimate an environment as the family at a time when we thought the races could not get much further apart (mid-1960s). To the best of our ability we sought the truth. We think we found it, as far as that abstract can be found. Over time, our work has withstood the public's test and various professions' scrutiny. We have written scores of articles and papers, been interviewed on radio and television, debated on panels, acted as pro bono consultants to all types of organizations, and been called upon as "expert witnesses."

What we have found is that in the overwhelming majority of cases, transracial adoption is a win-win situation. The child emerges a highly intact adult, aware of and sensitive to all areas those in opposition to TRA warned for decades they would be missing. The adoptive families exit with the knowledge that they have nurtured a productive member of society, at ease in a multi-racial world.

The opportunity now exists for social work to incorporate research findings about transracial adoption into practice and define TRA as one in a series of legitimate options available to parentless minority children. The challenge for adoption agencies is to overcome their apprehensions about not being politically correct, to do the right thing by examining the data, to adhere to the law, and to recognize that the data have been politicized by the rhetoric of some detractors. It does not seem farfetched to suggest that most agencies do not put research findings into practice for fear of being termed racists.

We strongly urge child welfare agencies to examine the empirical work. Scrutinize the data that speak to the adoptees' relationships with their adoptive parents, siblings, extended family members, and friends. Look at how they see themselves as human beings; as blacks, Asians, Indians; as men and women. Evaluate the fact that the overwhelming majority are comfortable in their chosen professions and worlds, that the explosive rhetoric of those who so strongly opposed TRA has not been realized. Determine agency policies and practices from the vantage point of science rather than fear. To reject sound information because it would aggravate certain groups is anathema to any profession, particularly social work, because we have so few long-term studies upon which to base our practice. To reject any data on other than scientific grounds weakens the legitimacy of any profession—again, specifically social work—for the reasons cited previously.

As we head toward the twenty-first century, the future of transracial adoption sadly appears to be a reflection of the past. The prospects of achieving permanent nurturing environments for the thousands of minority children legally free for adoption seems bleak if steps are not taken to have them permanently placed. Permanency can be accomplished in two ways: (1) by recruiting enough racially similar families willing to adopt these children, with or without subsidies, or (2) by allowing racially different families to adopt these children. We see no other solutions at this time.

Although it has been thirty years since we first contacted the families in our longitudinal study, we think it is worth repeating the final message that emerged from our first set of interviews with the parents. When we asked them, "If a family like your own, in terms of religion, income, and education living in the community, asked you to advise them about whether they ought to adopt a nonwhite child, what would your advice be?"[5]

Over 90 percent (7 percent said as a matter of principle they would not advise anyone on such an important personal decision) said they would urge the family to go ahead and adopt.[6] Most of them also emphasized that the parents' decision must be made on the bases of how much they wanted a child and because they believed they could offer the child a good home. "Slogans, causes, and political ideology should have no place in their decision." Most of the parents mentioned bad motives such as "proving you are liberal," "wanting to do something noble," or "taking a stand against the population explosion." The good motives were the "selfish ones, including wanting a child very badly."[7]

In all of our subsequent encounters with the families, the advice remained the same. Yes, adopt; but do it because you very much want a child and believe you can give him or her a caring, stable home.

If a "child's best interests" and his or her "least restrictive placement" corollary are to be serious practice foundations, then children legally free for adoption who are trapped in America's foster care system should be adopted by families willing to provide those children with loving homes . . . inracial or transracial. To do anything less for these children is not only to doom them to what we know does not work, but to deprive them of rights as citizens as called for in the Fourteenth Amendment to the U.S. Constitution, "No State shall . . . deprive any person of life, liberty or property without due process of law; nor deny to any person within its jurisdiction the equal protection of the laws."

NOTES

1. Matching was the long-held social work practice of attempting to duplicate an adoptee's physical characteristics with those of the adopting parents.

Thus, a blond, blue-eyed, fair-skinned infant would only be placed with a similar-appearing set of parents.

2. Joyce Ladner, "Bring Back the Orphanages," *Washington Post,* October 29, 1989; Richard O'Mara, "Are Orphanages Better for Kids Than Welfare?," *Baltimore Sun,* November 27, 1994, p. 1F; Katharine Q. Seeley, "Orphanage Revival Gains Ground," *New York Times,* December 20, 1997, p. A8; Joyce Ladner, *Mixed Families* (New York: Doubleday, 1997), p. 254; "Orphanages Are No Solution," *New York Times,* December 12, 1994, p. A18; "The Orphanage Option," *Washington Post,* Editorial, April 24, 1994, p. C6.

3. *Foster Care, Implementation of the Multiethnic Placement Act Poses Difficult Challenges.* GAO/HEHS-98-204, September 1998, pp. 1, 11.

4. Judith K. Mckenzie, "Adoption of Children with Special Needs," in *The Future of Children,* Center for the Future of Children, vol. 3, no. 1 (Spring 1993): 72.

5. Rita J. Simon and Howard Altstein, *Transracial Adoption* (New York: John Wiley & Son, 1977), p. 105.

6. Ninety-one percent of the respondents in the Grow & Shapiro survey also said they would urge both white and black parents to adopt transracially. Grow and Shapiro, op. cit., p. 85.

7. Simon & Altstein, op. cit., p. 106.

Index

About the Authors

Rita J. Simon is a sociologist who earned her doctorate at the University of Chicago in 1957. Before coming to American University in 1983 to serve as dean of the School of Justice, she was a member of the faculty at the University of Illinois, at the Hebrew University in Jerusalem, and at the University of Chicago. She is currently a "University Professor" in the School of Public Affairs and the Washington College of Law at American University.

Professor Simon is the author and editor of numerous books and is currently the editor of *Gender Issues.*

Howard Altstein earned his B.A. from Brooklyn College in 1959 and his M.S.W. in 1962 from New York University. He has worked as a social worker in corrections, foster care, and education. After receiving his Ph.D. from the University of Illinois at Urbana in 1971, he became a lecturer at the Hebrew University School of Social Work. He has been with the University of Maryland School of Social Work since 1972, and is currently a professor, having served as dean for one year.

Professor Altstein is the author of several books on transracial and intercountry adoption. Two additional books are forthcoming.